MY LIFE

MY STORY

MY JOURNEY

& A TALL TALE

{BOOK TWO}

-MY PILGRIMAGE CONTINUES-

-RBK

AN

R

B

K

READ

-FOR THERESA-

TABLE OF CONTENTS

AUTHOR BIOGRAPHY

R.B.K. has been an introverted rebel his entire life. A custom motorcycle builder and tradesman from northern Alberta, Canada he travels his spiritual path daily. An indie Author and Poet, he has published two books and continues to write. Documenting his own twin flame journey. Within the solitude he enjoys, he ponders the lunacy of man and if you asked him, what was life like before insanity? He would answer. You tell me! The most down to earth person you could ever meet. Having been there and done that. His pilgrimage has led him here!

INTRODUCTION

Dear reader,

As my spiritual ascension continues, I follow my twin flame path. Written in real time, this second book in the series explores my personal character in more detail. Exploring my world away from the retail outlet. Revealing how my awakened soul took flight and guided me toward the light. From high above in the crow's nest, my soul has directed my path, guiding me every step of the way and has led me to greater understanding and clarity. Leaving me centered with a sense of inner peace. Holding space for Theresa as I continued toward the junction of two paths.

My story continues within a story inspired by true events and real people. Included are some of my actual dreams, within the spiritual a hint of the mystical and a wee dash of fantasy. I have continued my story as the character KR and hope that these pages will shed some light on an ordinary man. One that was introduced to his authentic self while embracing the other half of his soul with unconditional love for all eternity.

-RBK

Book Three is included among these pages and continues to foretell my pilgrimage as I continued my journey further. Written once again in real time and in the present tense.

Part Two

MY PILGRIMAGE CONTINUES

ONE

SPRING – EQUINOX

{20-20}

A cold sweat had awakened him once again, the same vivid dream. Reaching for the Perrier beside the bed, he gulped down some water. Lying down, he drifted off to visit the sandman once again. Waking at sunrise, he recollected the dream while indulging in a cup of green tea, poaching two eggs and loading the toaster with whole wheat bread.

Standing in front of a locked lych gate, recognizing a familiar path leading toward a junction. The movement of a faint shadow is observed. The gate keeper is nowhere to be found.

The eggs were ready, along with peanut butter; jam on toast and a large glass of milk. While ingesting the breakfast, he could not help but focus on the dream, chasing it down with the milk.

Rolling in around midnight from a three-day ride, KR was still tired and decided to unwind and chill.

Working on the chopper was always relaxing. The chain needed to be tightened and an oil change was due. It was that time of year when the V-twin could be heard near and far and wide. KR could tell the difference between the old and new motors. Old-school simplicity was his motto, preferring to build his own, service and ride them.

Having a reputation for simplicity and perfection in building and pulling wrenches. There was always riding, cabbage in his pocket, and a part-time job creating some extra.

Washing some clothes while attending to some household chores, KR grew tired and decided to have a siesta before working on the chop. The lazy boy would suffice. Sinking into his favorite chair, he drifted off to visit the sandman yet again and once again visited the lych gate.

Stirred to consciousness by the sound of a shvl head motor, he smiled and exited the lazy boy. He opened the back door as a custom FXR rolled up the drive. Ramrod! The motor was hot from being run hard and it needed a break.

Not many bikers used the shvl anymore. Production had been stopped in 1983, but anyone who did use one knew why. The RUBs didn't have a clue, as they were only interested in the Harley's enigma, never understanding the culture. RUBs were instant bikers weaned while watching TV shows like Sons of Anarchy and American Chopper.

Ramrod and KR were old school through and through, society's stereotypes riding Harleys before it was cool. They were friends for years and never paid attention to anyone on two wheels wearing running shoes.

Ramrod hit the kill switch, shutting down the shvl as a billow of heat dissipated as it cooled. Sliding from the saddle, he stood and embraced KR - it had been a long while. Their conversation continued from where their last one had ended. Innis & Gunn was always in the fridge and KR offered Ramrod one.

There was a lot to catch up on but the trivial would have to wait. More important topics would commence first. What was being rode and built? And the second most important topic was women.

Ramrod opened another Innis. KR had never been a big drinker, eventually quitting the beer and only indulging in wine now and then.

KR loved to create, and building motorcycles was second nature to him. Living alone gave him the time needed to build. Having a new build ready to ride was important while riding another. There was always another build in progress. Questions were answered. Ramrod had a build on the go, and another Innis was opened.

The second topic was a little sensitive, both men learning to live with their mistakes. KR had kept women at arm's length for the longest time but recently not so much. Playing the field was what Ramrod did best. The trivial was conversed throughout the evening as they listened to music and broke bread.

As daybreak crept through the curtains you could hear the shvl fire up with a strong growl from custom-made straight pipes. The shvl was topped up with some oil, and Ramrod suited up with boots, chaps, a leather jacket, and finally his beany and glasses.

He rolled down the driveway, clutch pulled in, and the pipes were warm. Releasing the clutch, Ramrod headed south, twisting the wick. The 103-cubic inch stroker thundered through the crisp spring air, disappearing like lightning. It had been a memorable visit and they looked forward to the California trip that was planned together the previous evening.

Maintenance was still needed on the chopper, and KR had plenty of time before his five-hour shift started. Working part-time at the retail outlet put more riding cabbage in his pocket and of course, there was Theresa.

Slipping into a pair of older than new Denver Haynes, KR entered the tranquility of his shop. The chop always received the TLC required and in return always came through. Growling on the hard top, the pan always ran strong and was his favorite. Not many could understand his obsession with the old motors, but he didn't care. The original four motors had been tried and tested; simplicity was the key in a breakdown situation.

Checking his pocket watch, he realized it was time to go. As he prepared for work, he glanced in the mirror. The reflection had changed - not the facial features but something else.

The new build consisted of a spaghetti frame manufactured in California by Atlas frames. The heavy-wall one-inch tube was old school all the way, hard tail of course. Thirty-eight-degree rake, ten inches over in the down tubes, six inches added to the backbone, one inch more to the seat post. Spoked wheels, duel-disk four piston calipers mounted to a twenty-one-inch front wheel. Sixteen-inch rear wheel and four piston caliper. Five speed transmission with taller gears. Motor to be run – a 103-cubic inch cone knuckle with extensive work! The date for the California trip would be scheduled at the next drop by.

It ended up being a wonderful day, not a cloud in sight and 69 degrees. KR recalled the visit from Ramrod while wrenching on the pan so it would be ready to rock for the next rip. A five-hour shift and the sight of Theresa would round out the day superbly. Theresa made KR feel at ease, he enjoyed her company and was happy to call her a friend and his intuition apprised him of something mystical: she was one of those broads that just draws you in. The Innis & Gunn would need to be stocked up!

The evening was warm with a slight breeze adding some crisp air - all the ingredients needed for a ride. KR suited up as the pan was warming. He strapped on the lid, slid into the saddle, pulled in the clutch, loaded up first gear and headed west. He received an earshot of valve float as the pan red-lined between shifts, asking for more at 110.

He backed off the throttle as a favored terminus entered his sight: Green Grass Cemetery. KR pulled in the clutch, found neutral and coasted toward the gate. No gate keeper. Opening the lych gate, he recollected his dream as he entered.

Tranquility was always found there. Peacefulness was abundant and time endless. He had always found cemeteries alluring. The sun played peek-a-boo with the clouds, periodically casting a ray of light toward the earth and warming the ground. KR found a place to sit and rest, grounding himself with Mother Earth. He closed his eyes and visualized the enchanting smile he had received earlier that day. With a slight sigh, he smiled to himself.

As the sun set and the moon made its appearance, the pan was growling down the hard top. He was heading toward the Tower & Crown, a local pub where the food was exceptional, the bangers and mash anyway! The pan came to rest in front of the main entrance, pipes hot and the oil thin. Leaving his beany on the solo seat, KR entered and found his stool not taken. He ordered the mash and a Classic, knowing the day was about finished.

No one ever bothered him. KR was the typical stereotype who seemed to have travelled seven decades into the future. Carrying a seventy-year-old pocket watch and utilizing motors not in production did attract attention, but only from interesting people.

Finishing his plate, he swallowed the remains of the Classic, paid his tab and vacated the pub. He ignited the pan for a warm-up and engaged a hot little number in conversation while waiting. He slid her his business card, saddled the ride and idled toward the interstate. The brisk ride home was invigorating, and soon enough he arrived at his shack.

Home was a sixty-year-old bi-level with detached garage, considered a shack by the yuppies, only to be demolished and rebuilt. Bought and paid for, it was dry and warm. KR called it home and its door was always open.

Preparing for some shut-eye, KR warmed up the turntable and gently placed a blues album on the platter. The blues make the world feel so much more real. As side B finished, sleep was needed.

Crawling under a feather tick that his grandmother made by hand years ago made him feel tranquil. Slipping into the clouds, he floated into slumber. Tossing and turning throughout the night, he found himself standing in front of the lych gate, locked once again. The gate keeper was nowhere to be found. Peering through the gate just beyond the junction, he observed a rope bridge crossing a deep chasm. The bridge was lighted throughout its length. At the portal of the bridge, a silhouette was holding a lantern hanging from a crook, beckoning him to approach.

Staring at his reflection the next morning and trying to make sense of his dreams, he put them on the back burner and concentrated on the build. He would take advantage of this day off and create. The solitude was overdue!

A miserable day was waiting on the other side of the door: a light drizzle, broken-up clouds and a cool 60 degrees. Sliding the key in the shop door, KR entered his own little heaven. Some machining was first on the list. The shop was a builder's dream with all the needed tools: a lathe and milling machine, welder, drill press, oxyacetylene torch, tire machine, hand tools and more. Collecting tools for the shop was ongoing.

Throughout the day KR was focused on the task at hand, concentrating on the build. While he was savoring a cup of Earl Grey, a reflection of Theresa appeared behind his eyes. Taken back by the vision, he sipped the tea, envisioning a midnight rendezvous. He stepped outside for a breath of clean air as the sun was making an appearance. The pan would roll later.

The build was progressing. The tins were ready for paint, black of course, and the oil tank was ready for powder coat. Over the years the shop had been stocked and parts were on hand and ready to install.

Finishing up his day in the shop, he headed in for supper. The slow cooker had been busy all day working its magic on a blade steak. Baby carrots and onion were also included in the mix along with a potato. A side of corn would round out the meal, ending with a cool glass of milk chased by another.

What a pleasure it would be to break bread with his new friend, he thought, waiting for his tea to cool.

With a belly full of grub and the pan warming, KR suited up for a rip. He was still dialing in the new lock-up pressure plate installed earlier in the season and was anxious to test a new setting. He straddled the pan, slid into the saddle, released the clutch and headed west.

Merging onto Gibbon Ray Drive, he could feel the pressure plate doing its job. With a slight grin, KR twisted the wick and let the valves float between shifts, the drive train hooking up better than ever. Further testing would need to be done, assuming some new black top could be found.

Glancing in his rear view, he noted a newer model gaining ground. Dropping from five to three was an easy feat for the pan. With a snickering growl, the red line jumped, turning on the pan. Eighty … ninety … one hundred still pulling - the rear-view empty. Backing out of the throttle and making a left turn into St Peter's Graveyard, a running-shoe rider whizzed by. Speaking under his breath, KR said, "He sure could use some pipes!"

Having a fear for speed separates the experienced from the novice riders. Maintenance and awareness are key factors to survival.

St Peter's was another favorite stop. As the sun started to set, KR took a load off, sat back and reflected on the day as the sun set, speculating on what tomorrow would usher in. He was reminded that women could still stir his soul, one anyway! It was getting late and time to head home.

Sunset ushered in the night, and with the added cloud cover, dark was the night. KR hit the road, but backing out of the throttle was his motto at night. Abruptly exiting the shadows was a porcupine – shit! Grabbing third gear and leaning to the left, he gracefully piloted the pan around the obstacle as the rear tire collected some quills. With his heart racing, KR continued homeward.

Entering the city limits, he decided to stop at the Tower & Crown before heading home. A bowl of hot soup sounded good. Rolling in the pan and coming to rest, he removed his lid and slid from the saddle. He recognized the hot little number from his previous visit; she introduced herself as he entered.

KR sat at a table this visit. Approaching his table, the hot little number from outside was Shawna Lee, who was an employee. She carried a large bowl of beef barley and a Classic. Spinning around and heading toward the kitchen, she strutted her stuff, glancing back in his direction.

One bowl was not quite enough, so he ordered a second. The thought of a beer simply vanishing like lightning put an end to his craving. It had been years and Innis was the only beer he would consume. The second bowl was up on deck, delivered with a smile along with the tab. On his way out, a spliff was offered but he turned it down and decided to ride for a bit longer.

The moon's waxing crescent was lighting up the sky. It would make for an enjoyable ride. The pan was eager and still warm. Riding south, KR found some fresh black top, making a mental note for a future visit. As the cool wind tossed his ponytail from side to side, the smoothness of the twin whispered a compelling question. What was life like before insanity? He had forgotten! But then again, every man had an answer! He would sleep in a bit and run some errands before his shift at work.

Viewing his reflection in the morning drew his awareness to the subtle changes occurring within his character. Subconscious or conscious, he welcomed the change and felt new beginnings ahead. He decided that walking to work would do him good and clear his head, so to speak.

Walking to work took him forty-five minutes, and crossing a footbridge along the way reawakened his dreams. He strode through the downtown core and across another footbridge. Climbing a grassy kopje, he found himself at work, pondering whether to ask Theresa out.

Six to ten p.m. was his scheduled shift. The walk was invigorating, and he contemplated some more, considering the weather of course. Theresa had already left but he would catch her on the flip side. He was apprehensive of the outcome. Stepping up to the plate was motto number three. But he had a good feeling overall.

Arriving home around eleven, KR felt a shiver of the blues heading in his direction. He poured himself a goblet of Merlot and watched the legs of the wine run down the inside of the long-stemmed goblet. Captain Fantastic and The Dirt Brown Cowboys serenaded him to sleep. Drifting into the world of dreams, he found himself yet again in front of the lych gate. The falling goblet hitting the floor stirred him from sleep. He stumbled off to bed until sunrise.

Sunrise brought with it an early morning shift from seven till noon. KR decided to walk once again. Early morning dew was evaporating as the crisp air warmed. He would use the same route, keeping to the trails and out of traffic. As he was nearing the two-way cross walk, a chance meeting with Theresa occurred. He thought to himself "How convenient."

She lived in the surrounding neighborhood and would occasionally walk to work. KR was euphoric - what a great start to the day, answering his question with a yes! Theresa and KR shot the breeze just like two long-lost friends, separated for centuries. Feeling a connection of some sort, reminiscent of the past, he finished his shift.

The pocket watch indicated one p.m. Installing and balancing two tires would take the rest of the day. He procrastinated awhile, and then proceeded to the task at hand while enjoying some Black Foot played loud. His friend Psycho would be stopping by in the morning to pick up the tires. With the task finished KR could smell the cabbage rolls cooking. His stomach was growling and he dived right in, rounding out his evening with Nietzsche and some Merlot.

He received a text before sunrise. Psycho was en route. It would take him at least an hour. Wakening from his slumber, KR felt the cobwebs within, and lacking sleep, he decided to taper off the Merlot.

Psycho blasted in like a spaceship in one of those big-tired trucks that take a stepladder to enter. He fell to the ground from the driver's seat with a grin from ear to ear. He stood five foot six in black leather boots, cracked a beer and smiled. As the sun reflected off his stainless rings, he sat down to bullshit.

Psycho was a little rough around the edges with a heart as big as a bear. He was always there to lend a helping hand when needed. While loading the tires, he slid KR some cabbage, mentioned his interest in the California trip, and then blasting off, he disappeared.

A lingering sense of melancholy was in the air this particular day, and KR felt an urge to visit an old friend. He would plan a day trip for Saturday, leaving early and returning that evening. For the couple-hundred-mile round trip he would ride hard and fast, keeping the wind at his back. The pan needed some consecutive hard miles. It would be a good test for the new pressure plate. He sent a text and the return reply was "the door is open."

Hitting the road early, just as the sun started to rise, was beautiful, reminding him of Theresa as the crisp air hit his face while the thump of the twin led the way. Heading north with the wind at his back, KR added more fuel. The Harley ran well within its power band between eighty and a hundred, never grumbling when more was needed.

Entering Beaver Lake County with the city behind him, he needed a fuel stop. Never going below half a tank was motto number four. He added ten dollars of high octane, engaged first and headed north. Accelerating, he noticed red and blue lights up ahead. A roadside check stop. Turning left on a ridge road, he detoured the check stop and accessed the highway further north.

LANDING, population twenty-five hundred, one mile ahead. It was a sleepy little town built on one side of a gorge. The Acheron River flowed through the center, a ferry being the only way to cross. Nobody ever used it, but the ferryman was always on duty. Fuel would be added before the visit.

Wolf was an old school Ukrainian. Never afraid of hard work, he made his living building log cabins, harvesting the logs from inherited land, and his business thrived. He shipped cabin packages all over the country and became very prosperous. Never forgetting his roots, he was still a very humble man. Retiring to a life of solitude and exploring the lunacy of man, he was wise beyond his years.

22

KR rolled into the drive, shutting down the pan and receiving a bear hug from Wolf. They headed indoors to break some bread. Lunch had been prepared and the table was littered with Ukrainian favorites: dill pickles, ham and garlic sausage, beet soup, cheese, fresh baked bread, pickled fish, and poppy seed loaf. They washed it all down with a shot of shine. Taking a load off in the den, they listened to the latest Helix release. Sipping on some Earl Grey, they shared stories from the past. Having a pull from an oil joint, they sat back and relaxed.

KR checked his pocket watch; it was 4:20 p.m., time to roll. He suited up while the pan warmed. Wolf said "Don't pay the ferryman until he gets you to the other side!" Fueled up and ready to rock, KR released the clutch and headed south.

Visiting his old friend did him good. He added fuel to the Super G, and the hard tail effortlessly hauled its passenger home. The frequency of the pan head was meditating. Feeling Theresa enter through the back door of his mind, he smiled as he shifted into fifth.

TWO

MIDNIGHT

KR ended his day with Nietzsche and a cup of goat weed tea, reflecting upon his day. With a sigh, he swallowed some tea and continued to read, acknowledging Nietzsche as one of the greatest minds in history. He drifted off to sleep.

As his eyelids flickered open, a new day had begun. Destiny had scheduled a midnight rendezvous, just like you would read in a novel. KR was ecstatic and could not wait. His whole day was spent working on the new build, counting the hours and daydreaming until the hour was near.

The Tower & Crown was not far. He decided to walk so he could clear his head and relax. Arriving early, he sat at the bar with his back toward the door and waited. Checking his pocket watch, he saw it was twelve sharp! The door swung open as he turned, and Theresa was walking toward him. Throwing her arms around him, she whispered in his ear, "happy to see you." It was surreal! This was life before insanity! Question answered.

His soul had been shaken and stirred by this strange connection and wanted more. She was an enigmatic part of his puzzle, but where did she fit in?

THREE

ENGINES

A beam of sunlight travelling through an opening in the faded curtains bounced off KR's eyelids, blinding him for a moment in the darkness of his basement. Rolling over onto his back, stretching and yawning, he smiled to himself, reliving the past evening's rendezvous. Directing his size twelves to the floor, he arose and started his day. He cranked up some Black Foot, ascended to the main floor and contemplated some breakfast. A grapefruit, a slice of whole wheat bread and a cool glass of whole milk would hit the spot. Having the day all to himself, he relaxed after his meal and decided the next step on the build.

While washing the dishes he daydreamed of a new residence that was in his future plans, but that would have to wait until after the California trip. The focus now was the build. Ramrod was in builder's mode and a complete chop would have to be ready for the trip. With his build progressing well, KR sat back in the lazy boy for a moment and reflected on the direction of his life. He wondered where it would lead, and hoped somehow that Theresa would be included.

Sliding on his old new Denver Haynes and opening the side door, KR stepped out into a wonderful warm day. He prepared to install some ape hangers onto the build and dreamed once again of a new residence, far away from the rat race and noise created by man's lunacy. His perception and intuitive nature had begun to sharpen. While he was proceeding to the shop, the flip phone sounded.

It was a text message from Ramrod. "Heading to Beaker's tomorrow, interested? Pick you up ten sharp!" KR returned a text, "Hell ya!"

Beaker, a superb motor builder had been around for quite some time. Growing up in the day of the pan head, he had seen it all. The evolution of the Harley engine did not impress him. Known for his techniques in old school motor building, Beaker had a reputation second to none on the racetrack.

Rolling up the drive at ten sharp, Ramrod was like a kid in a candy store, so excited that his motor was finished. This motor was an upgrade from the previous one and would turn some heads. Five-inch stroke, high compression, hand-machined Leipheimer camshaft running solid lifters. That would make any Harley engineer quiver. Heading south-east on hi-way fourteen, Ramrod and KR settled in for some BS between old friends. Discussing the California trip and considering adding Psycho to the roster, after all he was interested.

Rainwright was a larger hamlet filled with down-to-earth people that seemed to have just been planted there. It was a community where everyone looked out for each other and the lunacy of man was a far distant rumor. Streets rolled up by nine and the stillness of the night washed over the sleepy little town until sunrise.

The hamlet was nestled in an old river bed where, over the years, the vegetation had taken over. The different colors of green foliage, spruce and poplar trees, camouflaged the hamlet from the clouds above. Entering the limits, Beaker's shop came into view. Ramrod could not wait and anticipated the beauty of the shvl engine that very few acknowledged.

As they entered Beaker Cycles their eyes caught a glimpse of the motor, nestled in a motor stand and all ready to go. Sensing the eminent power of the old school motor, Ramrod was delighted. Beaker cracked some beers and they sat down to shoot the shit - motors were the topic.

The cooling liquid made the conversation continue until closing. Beaker had reminded KR about his motor and assured him all was on track and completion would be soon. Some parts had been back-ordered but there was no need to hurry. One should never rush a motor build. Finishing up the conversation, they loaded the motor and a meal was planned at the Honey Pot.

Both being famished after a long day of travel and conversation, two porterhouses had been ordered, one well done and the other rare. KR opted for the well done. They also ordered baked potatoes with all the garnishes, a side of green beans and garden salad. Coffee and tea were ordered, along with some mineral water and some milk for KR's addiction. Conversation included the thought of one more addition to the trip now that Psycho had signed up, and KR had a bro in mind, increasing the count to four. Rounding out the meal with some bread pudding, the two of them filled up while Ramrod indulged in a joint.

The return trip was filled with some basic trip planning but they would have to get the four together to merge some ideas. Psycho was amid a motor change and would be ready in time. Replacing Harley's Evolution motor for a shvl was no surprise and Psycho would be impressed. After a test riding a shvl, Psycho was sold on the bottom end torque and needed to have one. Installing the motor in a FLSTN Nostalgia was a good choice and KR could not wait to see the finished product.

Arriving home before midnight, KR would wait and contact Lurch in the morning. He hoped he would be interested in the trip and it would be great to ride beside him again. The sandman was closing in - time to crash.

Lurch was one of KR's oldest and dearest friends, a soul mate. They had travelled many miles together within many lifetimes. KR was a very spiritual man and felt alone at times in our society. Lurch understood and could relate to the spirituality that surrounded KR. Feeling at ease around each other, conversation was always about the metaphysical.

Solitude was equally important to both of them. Living in the wooded back county of Barwell and operating a heavy-duty mechanical shop, Lurch prospered and KR took every opportunity to visit in the riding season. Sitting around open fires listening to Skynyrd was a summer occurrence. With barbeques, beer and a joint or two, they would be friends until the next incarnation. Old souls both learning and advancing after each incarnation. These two friends understood the bigger picture and sought out more understanding as the years passed them by. WISDOM IS THE UNDERSTANDING OF SILENCE. Many nights were spent pondering these words while birch and poplar burnt to ash and floated away with the wind.

The Pan Head was the third of the original four Harley engines and Lurch's favorite, so of course he had one. Now this motor was something special, not typical by any means. To get the motor assembled, machined and numbered, Lurch designed the pan using old and new technologies. At ninety-eight cubic inches, this build would pull more torque than Ramrod's 103. Four old school engines on the trip, maybe!

Through the grapevine Lurch had heard a rumor of the California trip and when KR asked him, he accepted the invitation. The trip would last about six weeks and all four motors would be broken in on the trip. With all said and done, four confirmations for the trip were finalized. All builds would have to be roadworthy within the year.

The early morning had brought cloud and rain. First just a light drizzle, but thunder could be heard in the far distance and intuition forecast a storm on the horizon. KR had felt a change within himself since meeting Theresa. Gazing in the mirror each morning, he concluded she was some sort of catalyst, propelling him to venture further into the realms of his spirituality. Starting to dabble with meditation, he became more grounded and still within. Giving him a sense of oneness, he explored it further. With the thunder growing louder and the rain heavier, it was a perfect time to catch some shut-eye. Opening the window a hair, KR slid under the feather tick and closed his eyes.

Breathing in the cool air and with the thunder shaking the ground, wrapped in the feather tick he drifted off to sleep. Climbing toward the lych gate once again. The flip phone bounced around, his eyelids slammed open. He was wide awake. Psycho needed some help. His motor was ready to install.

Vodka was his drink of choice, vodka and Coke that is. Psycho was a friend who dated back to childhood. Riding many miles together and sharing a similar upbringing, they worked hard and rode hard. Enjoying the wind and speed, living life to its fullest. Each living a different life but connecting with the road and the rumble of the greatest engine ever built.

Installing a motor into a frame can be a difficult job and a lot easier with two, and KR was happy to help. He entered the garage and they unbolted the motor from the stand. Together they slid the mill into the frame, both standing back and admiring the shvl, acknowledging it was the right choice. After a short visit KR returned home.

Entering his home, KR relaxed for a moment. He opened the fridge, assembled some leftovers from previous meals and sat down for supper. Embracing the change happening to him. Feeling it more and more each day. Welcoming it he pondered the result and how it would change him. Meditation had become part of his days and he enjoyed the peace it brought him. Knowing mainstream society would not understand, KR kept silent, conversing on the subject only with Lurch.

Wyatt was a riding companion from many years ago and had reappeared via a text message. Departing in separate directions, Wyatt and KR had not seen each other since the heyday of the eighties. Donning an MC cut, Wyatt became embroiled in the drama and intrigue of the club culture. Disappearing into Society's forgotten. KR answered the text "What's shakin?"

People come and go throughout one's lifetime, learning from each experience and then moving on to the next. There were a lot of acquaintances that had come and gone, and Lurch was the go-to. A soul mate travelling through time, keeping KR company. He was thankful for that. Sharing his spirituality and newfound changes were important to KR. A scary new adventure he wanted to explore.

Drinking a cup of goat weed tea, tiredness fell upon him as he reclined in his lazy boy, drifting off to his memory of the midnight rendezvous. Dreaming of another, his eyelids closed.

FOUR

OPEN-MIND

Feeling a newfound inner peace within himself, KR embraced it. Growing stronger each day, his heightened sense of intuition led him forward. Seeking out more awareness. Determined to create a new self. Continuing to keep it to himself, he would discard all that was of no use to him and all friendships that served no purpose. Stepping into a new dimension and reality manifesting all that he desired. A world free of lower vibrations.

Sylvia Browne had introduced him to the metaphysical and spiritual worlds years before, and Albert Einstein's quote "Imagination is more powerful than knowledge" resonated deeply with KR during this time in his life. Some books on quantum physics would be purchased to further his investigation. Hypothesizing that spirituality and quantum physics were intertwined together within the universe, and that all things were possible, leaving no stone unturned, he searched for answers. This led him to unchartered waters where he discovered that his hypothesis was correct.

We all live in different realities, only being aware of one. Our limited three dimensions keep us from being aware and seeing the others all around us. Changing the smallest thing within your now reality causes a ripple effect on all other realities. Each reality is constantly changing. Being awakened and embarking on a spiritual ascension, letting go of the lower vibrations and utilizing the higher ones enables us to travel from one reality to another within other dimensions. Manifesting our desires and living different lives. Being aware of the changes.

Analyzing the subject material and his inner self-changes, he concluded that his own reality had changed. Theresa opened the door to his new reality. Acknowledging it as he slid into his favorite chair. Opening a book of Karl Marx and recognizing this new reality, KR read on.

Karl Marx was ahead of his time. Living in the eighteen hundreds, he understood the manipulations of the capitalists and was aware of the internal conflict that would ensue between the ruling class and the working class. Capitalism would eventually self-destruct. One man's living should not be derived from another's labor. Marx has typically been cited as one of the principal architects of modern social science.

With his works influencing many worldwide. KR totally understood this philosophy and did question those who did not. Leaving them with the comment "Open your eyes and have a good look before closing them once again."

As he was closing the book, the flip phone had vibrated onto the floor. Picking it up, KR viewed a time-delayed text from Wolf. See you on the other side! I have saved some money for the ferryman and yes, I will not pay until I reach the other side. Later. Wolf was always curious about the other side of the Acheron River. Knowing that Wolf could take care of himself, he savored a cup of green tea, expecting a visit from Wyatt.

A distant rumble could be heard within the traffic - new age muffler systems designed for the high-end consumer that really did nothing for performance - just a high price tag. Handmade straight pipes were a far better choice and were more economical while producing more horsepower. A 2019 model rolled up the drive. One that blended in with the rest and had no character. Just like what the RUBs were riding. Wyatt was wearing a pair of Neil Young runners and was an absolute replica of a Sons of Anarchy character. Sporting a club cut he grinned from ear to ear.

Laughing at each other and recognizing how forty years had changed them both, they settled into reminiscing. Offering a beer, KR engaged the conversation with "How are Harley's new technologies?" Shrugging his shoulders, Wyatt complained "Not worth a shit," realizing that the simplicity that came along with the old was still more efficient. The bigger inch motors nowadays were just a selling gimmick that the RUBs ate up as evolution, not understanding the whole concept of simplicity.

There was some stew in the crock and KR invited Wyatt to break some bread. Wyatt remarked that one thing that had stayed the same after all these years was KR's hospitality and his cooking. Wyatt wasn't pleased with the direction the club culture had taken. The egos and attitudes of the new generations were unnerving at times and a new direction was needed. A step back into the past would guide his club back to old school values. Asking KR for his help, they broke some bread and continued eating. Acknowledging the request, KR said he would think about it. Retreating to the library for some vintage Merlot, the stories continued with a friendship rekindled.

With the red finished and the vanishing sound of the new age Harley blowing in the crisp night air of early spring, KR found himself alone. Living so many years within the confinement of solitude, he had forgotten the still of the night. His new friendship with Theresa had awakened the dormant feeling. Being completely aware of her role in his new reality, smiling he retired for the evening.

They had all met up at the Tower & Crown. Filling their bellies while swilling some ale. The main topic was the California trip. A lengthy ride like this should have some forethought and all four had agreed on some sort of a plan. The route would be simple. They would meet at Ridge Road 666 and from there head straight south on highway twenty-two. At Rock Bluff they would head west into the mountains, riding hard until they hit the border crossing at Blue Rock. Once in Washington State, they would roll down the coast to California. Keeping the wind at their backs they would never ride a head wind.

Packing light with only the essentials, camping would be the main objective. Renting rooms only in the case of wet weather. Cooking over an open flame and sleeping on the ground would make the trip more realistic. Stepping into a long forgotten iconic culture that films like Easy Rider and Hells Angels 69 had depicted. This was nothing new for the posse. All agreeing, refreshments were ordered and the natter continued. Shawna Lee hovered around while working, trying to get an ear full. After her shift she sat in for a drink.

KR was not himself and felt something was missing since entering the pub that evening. He knew what it was, kept it to himself and engaged in the chit-chat. The words "Happy to see you" flashed through his mind each time the door swung open. It had been a while since his one-hundred-and-twenty-day contract had ended.

Finishing the Classic and preparing to leave, KR wished Shawna Lee a good night and commenced his excursion home. The evening spent in the Tower & Crown had let the blues saunter around his aura. The lingering presence of Theresa compounded the need for meditation followed by some music. Speeding up the pace, he walked across the footbridge and into the park. While taking a break he glanced at the moon and envisioned his new life. With his reality changing, he headed home.

Adding stones and crystals to his daily meditations seemed to balance KR. It had been a while since their rendezvous. Knowing that some distance was a good thing, he still could not shake her presence, even away from the Tower & Crown. Flipping through some vinyl, he came across some Billie Holiday. Playing side two while sipping on a twenty-year-old Pinot Noir, he tripped back to the Eighties. Pablo's white always went well with red. The late seventies

Trooper's Thick as Thieves album was played, both sides of course.

The meditation along with the tunes had once again faded the color of blue and with the help of the red prepared KR to meet his dream-maker. Maybe a return to the lych gate could be arranged, but needing a key to enter was causing a problem. The recently cleaned feather tick would be appropriate for the coolness of the night. Soaring through the clouds of unconsciousness, sleep fell upon him.

Spending the day working on his build, KR envisioned the finished product and could not wait to install the motor. Knowing that in due time it would be finished, he continued the electrical wiring and prepared the seat for upholstery. Genuine leather would be used, none of this Naugahyde shit. That was just disrespectful. The tins were still at the painters. All in all, everything was on track. KR had always been well organized to the point of fanatical and in the end no one could disdain his building methods. Having prepared a meal earlier in the morning, KR looked forward to an evening meal and some solitude. Another meeting of the posse was to be held at the end of the week to discuss U.S entry. As he was preparing to have some windows and doors replaced, KR decided to lay low and continue his spring cleaning.

The week passed quickly and KR was kept busy with spring cleaning and garage duty, while looking forward to a plate of bangers and mash chased with a Classic. Friday arrived and the pan was down for some maintenance. Turning down all invitations for a lift, KR opted to walk. The heat from the motors could be felt as he walked toward the entrance. All were in attendance and the sit-down could commence. Shawna Lee, of course, waited on the posse's table. Drinks and food were ordered and the get-together commenced.

Entering the U.S had changed, and a driver's license would no longer grant entry. Passports were now the norm. All riders retained one. Meeting adjourned.

Stepping into the entrance of his home, the flip phone vibrated out of his pocket and hit the floor. New text message: "Hey, you free for another rendezvous tomorrow night? Same time, same place? T." KR replied "c u then." Smiling as he stepped into the kitchen, he opened the fridge, poured some Perrier and sat down at the kitchen table to thumb through the latest issue of Iron Horse. He was beginning to like his new reality. Out with the old - in with the new. He glanced in the mirror while preparing for some shut-eye, acknowledging the changes from within.

He thought of his grandmother as he pulled the feather tick toward his shoulders. Lying back he noticed the dream-catcher hanging above. Maybe a dream could be caught tonight? He had not visited the gate for quite some time and felt there were some answers within the dream. Walking on a sea of sand, the sandman took his hand and he found himself at the edge of a forest. Running water could be heard in the distance. Following the sound, he came across a fast running brook. It was deep and the water so clear that the bottom could be seen. Small stones on the bottom reflected the sunlight piercing the surface. Taking a much-needed rest on a fallen tree, the peacefulness along with the running brook reminded him of no other place. As he enjoyed the serenity and a drink of water, from the corner of his eye he caught a glimpse of a fellow traveller walking toward him.

The traveller approached with caution, introducing himself as Plasoveus. He was a tall man with piercing eyes that looked right through KR, and a beard and long hair to match. Both were the brightest white he had ever seen, with a hint of silver highlighting his beard. He was dressed in a greyish white robe, tied at the waist with a hemp rope. Using a crook as a walking stick, he sat down on a fallen tree. Reaching into his rucksack, he retrieved a pint pot and filled it with water to quench his thirst. Drinking it quickly, he refilled it for one last drink. Opening the bum bag tied at his waist, he handed KR two crystals. One was Carnelian and the other Citrine. He said, "These crystals will open the gate. Follow the path north, then climb the ladder." With these few words he departed in the same direction from which he had arrived. KR felt a familiarity about Plasoveus, and as he headed north he wondered if he would ever see him again.

Beginning to narrow, scrub brush had overgrown the path making it difficult to proceed. Crawling on his hands and knees, the bottom of a ladder came into view and he stepped onto the first rung. His flittering eyelids opened and he glanced at the clock - 5:15 a.m. Then he rolled over to catch some more zees.

Awakening near noon, he stretched and yawned, then KR flung himself to attention. He had slept in and felt as though his day was wasted, but on the other hand, he accepted it for what it was. Looking forward to midnight with anticipation, he climbed the stairs and entered his kitchen.

A cup of Earl Grey to start the afternoon would curb his appetite. Bangers and mash were still on the menu and two orders were reserved for this evening with Classics on the side. With the pan still in maintenance mode, the afternoon would be spent installing a new drive chain and rounding out spring maintenance ready for the summer.

Using stones and crystals with his daily meditations, KR was familiar with Carnelian and Citrine. Separately they were used to balance and cleanse chakras and together they made powerful allies. Adding the two to his collection, he would always carry them. Crystals and stones were making their way into his new reality and KR felt very comfortable about it. They were bringing him peace and tranquility, keeping him centered and grounded, repelling negative energies, and cleansing his aura. While seeking out higher vibrations, letting go of the lower ones and feeling the change within, he persevered.

The pocket watch was set and wound three turns only. It had turned out to be a cool warm evening with a slight breeze. A blanket of see-through clouds set the stage for a starry night, reminding him of the Van Gogh painting. KR walked the familiar route, guided by the waxing crescent of the moon. Across the footbridge, alongside the river, and up a rocky hummock. The neon light of the Tower & Crown shone brightly, leading him home. Anticipation of the rendezvous increased with each step. As the big hand aligned with the small, midnight struck as he opened the door and stepped into his new reality.

The pub was nearly empty. Theresa was sitting at the bar, wearing her brown leather jacket. Spinning

45

around on the stool, her smile lit up the room. Her hair was down, with a strand hanging over her face. As she brushed it aside she said, "Happy to see you." Time stood still and the moment was real. They moved to a reserved table where three flowers were nestled in a vase: Azalea, Angelica and an Apple Blossom. All pertained to the heart, and in full bloom their aroma filled the air. There was a brief instance of silence and then their order was up. Breaking bread together had become a reality for KR. Savoring every moment as her energy engulfed his aura. Feeling that sense of home as he swallowed the remains of the Classic. Conversing until closing, time was irrelevant.

As the neon light flickered off, KR walked Theresa home under a starry night sky. With the remnants of snow from the previous winter, they exhaled a breath of fog, which danced on the crisp air until it vanished. After a warm embrace, Theresa smiled, "I'll see you soon."

FIVE

ZOMBIES

Spring maintenance had been completed on the pan. KR was considering a visit to the Smoking Aces clubhouse and gave Wyatt a heads up. The pan rolled down the driveway, barking in the crisp spring air. It was a little early for a ride but KR had been out several times already and would not lay into the throttle. Highway maintenance was still in progress and as safety was of the utmost importance, he opted for the longer route. Living his new reality, he mused on the self-changes and the sharp finger resting in his boot. The seven deadly sins all checked off except one. Old habits died hard. Advancing toward the clubhouse he overheard the gate keepers say, "Let the pan head in." An invitation was always a must.

As the chopper came to rest, KR dismounted and scanned the parking area. All newer models, one hard tail. Entering the remodeled garage all eyes focused on the stranger. Sitting at the bar beside Wyatt, the bartender served KR a Classic and introduced himself as Slim. Leaving some business cards at the bar, KR saddled up and entered the wind.

Over the years KR had worked hard on shedding his ego and keeping his attitude in check. The atmosphere in the clubhouse was so thick with egos and attitude that it could have been cut with his sharp finger. He would decline Wyatt's plea for help and distance himself from the club. Instead concentrating on the build and continuing his long-range plan to move. All the while hoping that Theresa would step into his reality more and more each day.

A move had been in his thoughts for years and now was the time to escape. Planning was essential and KR was exceptional at organization. The task would be completed within two years. His home had been retrofitted with new windows and doors, which would improve resale opportunities. New appliances would be installed along with a few simple upgrades. He planned on moving south-west to the next province where the weather would be milder. The weather would be welcomed along with a small-town atmosphere where the residents were not afraid to say good morning and the rat race was minimal or maybe even non-existent. De-cluttering had begun of all material items that served no purpose, as KR realized that the materialism of man literally served no purpose.

As a young adult entering the workforce KR was aware of man's lunacies and society's programming.

Living in the programmed world he functioned just like everyone else. Seeking answers through the philosophies and teachings of Nietzsche, Marx and even Freud. He began to unravel man's complex idealisms. Helping him to acknowledge his programming. He set forth to deprogram himself as much as possible - enabling him to see the world differently and more clearly - the bigger picture so to speak. This left him isolated from society's programmed followers at times - seeking solitude as his new friend, until the lit lantern led him home.

INSTILLED WITH GREED

BY THE GENERATION BEFORE

SET ON A PATH OF DESTRUCTION

OPEN YOUR EYES YOUNG CHILD

AND CHANGE THE WORLD

- RBK

SIX

FULL-SAILS

There was some snow remaining in the ditches and the weather was warming nicely. Yard work could commence further and KR felt centered and at peace with himself. Focused on the build, he would lean into summer with a full assault on de-cluttering, moving him closer to his long-range goal. Stepping ever further into his new reality, he felt that change was imminent. Living within the silence between the notes he grounded himself to Mother Earth, learning to live with the constant reminder of home.

KR despised yard work but did his best, keeping in mind the wise words of his grandfather, "Never pay anyone to do something you can do yourself." As he commenced with the task, a faint rumble could be heard. Far off in the distance - a block head from the evolution era. Growing louder and louder until a black hard tail came into view and rolled up his driveway. A block head nestled in an old wishbone frame from the knucklehead days. It was a nice build and he was impressed. Recognizing the rider, Slim was welcomed, KR offered him a beer and they sat down.

The Smoking Aces had been patched over by the Devil Dogs - the dominant club in the area. Slim wanted nothing to do with the club and parted ways. He'd left his cut on the table and was now looking for someone to ride with. Offering Slim an open invitation, they continued to discuss some machining which KR was happy to oblige with.

Rumor had it that Wyatt was to be set up as vice president of the Devil Dogs. KR knew with a strong sense of intuition that this was a bad move for Wyatt.

While searching for some aluminum to start Slim's project, KR heard the mailbox slam shut. He glanced through the garage door window as the letter carrier briskly walked away. Then, having found a suitable piece of metal to start the project, he decided to open his mail. Thumbing through mostly flyers of course, he noticed an unusual letter. He flipped it over, instantly recognizing the address - Calling Creek Reserve. Opening the letter, he discovered an invitation to the first annual sweat lodge gathering. It would be hosted by his old friend Six Owl aka Ray D. Ray who had studied over the years with many shamans and was helping people to access the spirit realms using peyote and ayahuasca. KR deciding to accept the invitation, hoping that the experience would help explain his dreams and enlighten his inner self.

Finishing a cup of back tea while the metal lathe warmed up, KR then proceeded to the task at hand. Within an hour Slim's machining was completed and KR sent a text of the news. Slim was en route and in what seemed like an instant, the black chop was parked on its side stand. Slim, with wrenches in hand, added the newly machined part. Satisfied with the finished product, some cabbage was placed into the shop's tip jar.

Relaxing in the back yard, sitting down and listening to the silence of the breeze whispering through the jack pines, KR mentioned the sweat lodge and asked Slim to come along. Slim agreed and late Friday afternoon they would meet at the Tower & Crown.

Friday peered through the clouds as the morning's first rays of light touched the earth. KR was excited to embark on a new adventure and welcomed what was to come. Riding with someone is great, but the thought of Theresa's hands wrapped around his waist lingered with him until breakfast. This would manifest itself when the time was right.

He was all ready to depart. The pan was mechanically sound with new tires, fresh oil and a new chain. With his bed roll tied and secured, leathers waterproofed, bike shined, saddle bag locked and loaded, he was to meet Slim at four p.m. He would do one last walk around and fire the pan. A good warm up was always important and a good practice to never forget. As he finished suiting up, he took a breath of fresh spring air and inhaled all its aromas, exhaling as he slid into the saddle.

Slim was already guzzling a cool one. A Classic was delivered along with Shawna Lee's smile as she tried to get their attention.

They would ride north to Landing, fuel up and have a meal at the Union Grand Hotel. Then proceed west following the Acheron River until they hit Calling Creek.

Riding side by side with KR at the center line, both riders were hypnotized by the sound of handmade drag pipes barking in their ears as the scenery passed them by. Leap-frogging the traffic, they entered Landing's town limits in good time, and parking in front of the Union Grand, they shut off the hard tails and went inside.

Entering the pub was like stepping back in time. There was an old wooden floor with peanut shells thrown about and wildlife hanging from the walls. Deer and moose antlers were used to hang jackets and the biggest set of elk antlers KR had ever seen was mounted above a Victorian pool table in very pristine shape. The Union Grand was owned and operated by the Calling Creek reserve. Martha May, the proprietor of the pub, leased the space from the reserve and while knowing everyone who passed through the doors, gossip and hearsay were her forte. Such as the latest about Wolf, who had climbed aboard the ferry, never to be seen again.

A buffet was offered. KR and Slim accepted and loaded up their plates. There was wild boar and deer venison - a slice of each - also roasted garlic potatoes, green beans and corn. They had two Classics on the side. Bread pudding rounded out the meal. KR finished his with a cool glass of white milk. An addiction he would carry to his grave.

The next leg of the trip would be to head straight west and ride with the direction of flow alongside the Acheron River. As the river turned north the reserve would be found hidden within one hundred thousand acres of forest.

Fueling up the hard tails, the river was a stone's throw away and the ferryman could be seen waiting for his next passenger. Stoking his fire to keep warm, his grey pale skin reflecting on the ripples of the river.

Turning north off the hard top, the road turned into a sandy trail amongst tall pines that had been around for a hundred years. Zig-zagging through the pines, they entered the reservation. Tossing out anchor at the main lodge, the hard tails came to rest. Ray D approached with a heartfelt welcome, inviting them to the fire gazing ceremony, which was about to start. KR knew the age-old tradition of fire gazing and he welcomed the invitation.

It had been a long day for the hard tail riders. Retiring to their accommodations, they lit a fire to warm the cabin and reminisced for a short while before the lantern lights dimmed. Both exhausted, they fell asleep as the arms of Morpheus engulfed them.

Sunlight bounced off the tops of the pines, sending splintering shards of light to penetrate the earth below. It lit up the darkness of the cabin and through an open window the faint smell of bannock cooking filled the air within, along with a trace of fresh jerky warming slowly over a small hickory fire. Breakfast preparations had begun and KR was famished. This would be a traditional Blackfoot breakfast and Slim was all in. This would be the last meal until after the sweat lodge. An empty stomach was needed for the ceremony.

KR had spent some time on the reservation in the past and was quite familiar with their customs and way of life. After showing Slim around for most of the day, KR decided to take a catnap.

He tossed and turned with visions that seemed to explode and then disappear right behind his eyes like a flash of napalm lighting up the sky, but behind a silk veil of some sort. The previous night's fire gazing had opened some sort of door through which he could see future events. Knowing that these visions were of importance, he kept the door open and would ask his friend Ray D for some help.

Both a bit nervous, Slim and KR were also excited and headed toward the sweat lodge. As they entered, the warm air was heavy and a slight mist filled the inside. Two hallucinogens were served. Ayahuasca, an entheogenic brew made from the banisteriopsis caapi vine and Peyote, a small spineless cactus that contained mescaline. Each of the hallucinogens had been made into a tea. Now these spiritual medicines have been used in traditional ceremonies for centuries and have entered the mainstream of today's society. As the teas began to be passed around the circle, KR took his turn swallowing a mouth full of each, then passed it on to Slim who grinned and gulped down his share. Leaning back with the sweat rolling down their faces, the ceremony began.

Feeling lightheaded and with his eyelids flickering, KR was still aware of his surroundings as he stepped through the veil. With his senses enhanced, he was in a 3-D reality much more profound than any previous dream. Feeling the sweat drip from his forehead, he wiped his brow and noticed Plasoveus from the corner of his eye. He was waiting for him at the edge of a forest.

The familiarity of the landscape was uncanny and at that moment KR remembered his previous visit. Walking closer to the forest, he heard the trickling brook once again. Acknowledging one another, Plasoveus and KR walked along the path in silence. The brook became louder with each step they took. They sat down to rest. KR's awareness was as sharp as a tack and he honed into each of his senses individually at his discretion. He quenched his thirst from the liquid of the brook. While relaxing for a moment, he shut his eyes for an instant and when he opened them, Plasoveus had disappeared, leaving him in the tranquility of Mother Earth.

With his honed eyesight, a silhouette of a woman came into view. Like the one he had seen at the lych gate, she was sitting on a fallen tree near the edge of the brook. She was holding a wooden bowl in her hands and using an aspergillum to sprinkle its contents into the water. She was observing the droplets as they danced on the rippling water of the brook before sinking like stones to the bottom. Then gazing upon KR as he came closer and whispering into the wind "if tears could talk, what would they say". With her crook and lantern, she disappeared under the lighted moon. Her last words "I'll see you soon" left him with that familiar sense of home.

Knowing the way out, KR found the ladder. Grabbing the bottom rung with two hands, he found himself inside the lodge as his eyelids fluttered open and a drop of sweat stung his eye.

The conclusion of the ceremony brought with it fatigue and an empty stomach. A light lunch was served followed by a relaxing soak in a nearby natural hot spring. The faint smell of sulfur lingering in the air made it feel more authentic. Tired from the day's experience, KR and Slim retired to the comfort of their accommodations, ending their day in complete wonderment of it all.

As the night sky brightened and dawn entered the horizon, the sun ushered in a new day. Shaking off the cobwebs while drinking some white tea, KR had surmised that the silhouettes in his dreams were the same person, conveying messages and leading him somewhere. The crystals he had received from Plasoveus would open the lych gate, enabling him to access the bridge on the other side. Perhaps this was part of the bigger picture and the silhouette would identify herself when the time was right.

As the hard tails warmed up, thank you's and goodbyes were exchanged. Ray D reminded KR that he would be in touch. Saddling up, the riders headed home with the roar and rumble of the V-twins left in their wake. The sunlight flickered through the pines and warmed their faces as they rode to the highway. Turning left and heading east on the hard top, the straight pipes barked and growled as their transmissions propelled the hard tails forward, the rpm of each engine in sync.

With the wind at their backs, Landing was not far. KR had to ask himself a question: "Could Theresa be the silhouette in his dreams?" His intuition confirmed it. Downshifting to fourth, the pan lurched ahead, then grabbing fifth, Landing was in sight.

Noticing the ferryman on the other side of the Acheron River picking up a passenger was unheard of, but two people were on board - the ferryman and someone else. With the hard tails full of fuel, they headed south, ripping up the main drag as the sun started to set. Side by side, they rode hard and fast until sunset, then the center line reflected the moonlight as it appeared. Stopping for a rest, they spilt a Classic and rolled a spliff. Still mystified about the sweat lodge experience, silence was heard.

At ridge road 222 Slim departed east. KR continued south, the pan digging into the hard top and that feeling of home overwhelmed him as he rode by the retail store. The presence of Theresa felt stronger than ever as he slowed for a traffic light. He pondered the thought of a return trip on the ferry. Was it possible? With the flashing green, KR exited left onto Gibbon Ray Drive and headed to his shack.

Sliding his key into the lock, he opened the door and stepped into solitude once again. His old friend that had kept him sane for years was always there when needed. The weekend spent at the reserve gave him a lot to think about. Lighting a fire, he sat down in the rocking chair that his mother had rocked him in as a baby. Reaching for a book, The Virtue of Selfishness by Ayn Rand, he opened it where the bookmark was left. Contemplating the selfishness of the world, he read on, and in wonderment asked himself a question: Is man aware of his selfishness concealed by his ego?

SEVEN

PINEAL GLAND

The Pineal gland. A pea sized conical mass of tissue located behind the third ventricle of the brain, and dubbed the third eye or the sixth chakra. Using light and sound meditations regularly will eventually open the third eye, heightening one's clairvoyance abilities, intuition, and higher consciousness. Within the mystic and esoteric spiritual traditions, it serves as a metaphysical connection between the spiritual and physical planes. Science does not fully understand its function but does confirm that the pineal gland produces melatonin, which regulates sleep patterns.

KR understood the metaphysical connection of the third eye and had experienced some visions brought on by the fire gazing ceremony. Wanting to explore the visions more thoroughly, he searched the web for new technologies. The Lucia light, developed in Austria by Dr. Proeckl and Dr. Winkler was advertised as "Hypnogogic light technology that will transport the attendee into the realms of the spiritual world." Contacting Ray D for some help, he found an answer.

A practitioner trained in the use of the light offered one-hour sessions for a reasonable price, and was based in a small town in British Columbia near the American border, close to where KR was planning to move.

This was exciting news. More clarity on his visions would help explain his journey and possibly shed some light, so to speak, on his friend Theresa who he had not seen or heard from for a while. A keen sense of intuition apprised him all was well, and she would reach out again in due time.

The Kootenay region of southern British Columbia, with its clear running streams, and lakes within forests of one-hundred-year-old trees, had a sparse population spread out among the towns and villages nestled within its mountain valleys. At the southern end of the province snow was a rare occurrence and temperatures were moderate to say the least. KR loved this area and had visited several times over the years. Deciding to relocate to a small town near the border. His dream was manifesting, and his new reality was in sight.

A solo trip was planned. KR would fly to Cranbrook where he would then rent a car and proceed to his destination – Yahk, a small village on the edge of a lake, a forty-minute drive from Cranbrook. The appointment had been made, flight arranged, car reserved and accommodations set. Departure was late afternoon on Friday.

After only an hour in the air, the plane touched down at the Cranbrook airport. Stepping onto the tarmac, KR took a deep breath. The air was so different in the mountains. Remembering that long forgotten smell, he exhaled and drew in another breath. The sun shone brightly in the sky warming Mother Earth. A seventy-degree day. KR was full of expectations of what the next day would bring.

He remembered a twenty-four-hour truck stop on the main drag, where he knew the food was good. He sat down and scanned the menu. Bangers and mash and a Classic on the side, and so it was. It was reminiscent of a previous rendezvous and a vision of her flashed behind his eyes.

Saturday morning came quickly. Still full from the night before, KR decided to take advantage of the continental breakfast offered with his accommodation. The Lucia light session was not until 1 p.m. There was lots of time to visit the local hot springs, relax for a while and breathe in some clean, fresh mountain nitrogen with a mix of oxygen.

Nakusp was one of those out-of-the-way places that everyone thought no one knew about, and called their own. Sitting on the edge of upper Arrow Lake, a town of only five thousand, large pines and spruce stood tall and shaded the lazy little town. It was a place where the inhabitants would gladly offer an acknowledging smile to all who walked the streets. KR had visited many times and always enjoyed the stillness of the silence in the area.

As the warm water touched his skin a slight breeze was felt, and a hint of sulfur lingered above the water's surface. Using some American Optical eye wear, KR leaned back and relaxed. Asking himself a question – who was the coolest - James Dean or the Fonz?

Tibetan meditation music filled the air, relaxing the patrons as they sat silently in the soothing water. KR took advantage of the moment, clearing his mind he focused on his new reality. Remembering Einstein's words "Imagination is more powerful than knowledge," he embraced his spiritual journey, letting the universe lead him. With a heavy sigh, he exited the pool.

Yahk was one of those places that if you didn't have business there you would drive right on by.

Small and secluded, it was a great place to do some soul-searching after a life lived in the programmed rat race, which the world acknowledged as "that's the way it is!"

House number 222. He checked his pocket watch, it was 12:50. Using the door knocker, KR waited. As the door opened, a tall and slender older gentleman answered with a warm smile. Introducing himself as Ivan, he invited KR in and they entered a sunken living room. It was filled with leather furniture dating back to the Fifties, the kind that psychologists would use. The Lucia light was hanging over a worn and tattered black leather couch. The room felt relaxing and comfortable, and feeling at ease in the presence of Ivan, they proceeded with the session.

Lying on the couch KR could sense its history. Closing his eyes and clearing his mind, the session began. The light patterns penetrated his eyelids until a white veil hung behind them. Staring at the veil for a moment, it began to open slowly like the curtains of an old theater. They revealed a long gravel driveway, fenced on one side, with a ground level log home in the distance and a two car garage. As the image drew closer, the inside view of the home was remarkable. There was a sunken living room with a loft and fireplace and a sliding rear door to the back yard, which had a view of the mountains. In the kitchen there was the silhouette of a woman looking through the kitchen window. A swing hung from the veranda, where there was a pair of rocking chairs with a table in between containing a collection of books.

The numeral 222 flashed as the curtains closed. As the curtains opened once again KR found himself riding the pan. In the distance ahead was an eagle soaring with the wind. A pair of hands was wrapped around his waist and he had that feeling of home snugly holding on. He admired the eagle as he rode, both free and content. Rounding a corner, there was a direction sign - Trail 222 km ahead. Thundering by the road sign, the curtains closed.

Ivan had prepared a light lunch of garden vegetables and fresh fruit, all organically grown in the area. Also a bowl of home-made beef barley soup, a slice of whole wheat bread and a Classic on the side. The chit-chat during the lunch included some history of the Lucia light and its technology. The recurring numeral 222 and its meaning, which KR was aware of from his information pursuit into the spiritual realms. As the lunch ended, Ivan poured two glasses of a vintage Pinot Meunier that would not be turned down. With the glass emptied, KR headed back to Cranbrook.

There had been a lot of information within the two visions and as he drove KR began to sort it out. The first being the numeral 222 and its meaning! HAVE FAITH. EVERTHING'S GOING TO BE ALL RIGHT. DON'T WORRY ABOUT ANYTHING, AS THIS SITUATION IS RESOLVING ITSELF BEAUTIFULLY FOR EVERYONE INVOLVED. Trail was to be the location of his new home. Thirdly, the silhouette in the kitchen and the passenger on the pan were Theresa. There was no doubt, and his intuition confirmed it!

The three hundred and sixty-five days between March 2019 and March 2020 had been extraordinary when compared to any before. Full of questions and unfamiliarity, each day dawned a new light on more questions. As KR followed his newly honed intuition, the reflection in the mirror began to change. Becoming aware of his new reality and the changes from within himself, his consciousness expanded and the world was a different place. Eager to control and then eliminate the seven deadly sins, he began to delete his ego. Realizing that this would be man's last stand and ultimately, the hardest thing he would ever attempt.

Theresa was the catalyst that propelled KR on his journey and he was now aware of her involvement. Although unbeknownst to her, she was in the passenger's seat for the long haul. Her energy and presence were felt twenty-four seven, entering his dreams while sleeping and thoughts throughout the days. KR became accustomed to the silhouette of his dreams, knowing that she would never leave. Fate had brought them together for a joint mission.

EIGHT

ANOTHER READING

Seat number twenty-two, a window seat near the back. Knowing that the tail of the plane is the safest, KR always sat in the tail section. Not that he was paranoid. Not at all. Just some valuable information he had picked up from his father who had owned and flown small aircraft over the years.

Adjusting his seat and finishing his Classic, he settled in for the short trip home. Contemplating another psychic reading, he had decided to explore his past lives, hoping to discover some valuable information that could be hidden in the past.

Sylvia Green, a reputable psychic had read for KR before. She understood his journey and had invited him back any time. Feeling comfortable with her, KR scheduled a reading. Taking a cancellation, the reading would take place within two weeks. This was great and his excitement grew as each day vanished one by one.

Sylvia had bought and remodeled a 1920's era home situated on a historical site two blocks from the river that flowed through the center of the city. Maples and Dutch elms fifty feet tall shaded the area like a thick fog. It was a brick and mortar house all refinished on the outside. Windows and doors had been replaced to the original style with added new technologies. A solid silver gargoyle door knocker hung from a solid walnut door finished with ash inlays. Crossing the threshold, it was unlike any other home, full of antiques spanning back two hundred years. Each antique had its own story to tell. A library filled with spiritual books of all kinds: Marks, Freud, and Nietzsche, including Ayn Rand - just to mention a few. All had found space on the shelves.

An oval mahogany pedestal table stood near one corner of the library. It was covered with white silk table linen, bordered with hand stitched brown and black lace. In the center of the table was a crystal ball and an assortment of other crystals had been placed within the library. An original 1930's chandelier hung over the table. Two leather chairs from the same era were placed around the table. A small fireplace added some elegance and simplicity.

Sylvia had a reputation for being somewhat eccentric and reclusive but KR was attracted to people who were different. It made them more real and earthly, unlike the facade of society's programmed followers.

Hypnosis was the tool used in past lives regression and Sylvia had mastered the art one thousand fold, proving repeatedly that incarnation was factual. While under hypnosis, the crystal ball was used to follow the client's vision and guide them as the vision progressed in the direction they wished to follow.

A red mahogany colored leather couch seven feet in length, with some goose down pillows and a wool blanket, rested parallel with the book shelf about six feet away. KR snuggled under the blanket and rested his head into the pillows, which reminded him of his grandmother's feather tick. Relaxing and clearing his mind, he sank deep into the comfort of the well-used couch and felt the warmth of the small fire lit in the fireplace while Sylvia prepared for the session.

A shard of black quartz swung back and forth in front of his eyes like a metronome's stick. His eyelids became heavy and darkness filled his vision.

Like a flash of lightning, a landscape lit up in front of his eyes. KR found himself running through a field of wheat five feet tall with an arrow through his left shoulder blade. Blood soaked his left side, his pace had slowed and he stopped for a brief instant to rest. His assailant was in pursuit. Recognizing his father as his master, he began to run faster and faster. With Sylvia's voice guiding him, he took refuge under a thicket and his assailant passed him by. Passing out from the lack of blood, KR then found himself on the couch once again. It was as if it had just happened - there was a slight pain in his shoulder blade and he felt tired from running. As he tried to make sense of this hypnosis therapy, he opted for some blueberry tea with a hint of Armagnac.

As Sylvia poured the tea and added the spirit, KR sat silently admiring her talents and gifts. Sipping the hot tea while indulging in a slice of poppy seed cake, Theresa's name entered the conversation.

While Sylvia was preparing the tea, Theresa's energy became present in the kitchen. Sylvia instantaneously heard her words, "KR and I have not seen each other for many lifetimes and a long term reunion is to happen. I will see him soon." As quickly as the energy appeared, it disappeared. The occurrence was nothing new to Sylvia and it proved the connection between KR and Theresa that he had felt for quite some time. Reeling in the newfound information, he reached for another slice of cake. After finishing the tea, KR then exited through the walnut door.

Every step taken in his search for answers was leading him closer to Theresa each and every day. No more stumbling in the dark. Information compiled over the last year had explained much and his direction was clear. Shadow work and daily meditation would help him remain grounded. Staying focused on his journey, KR would embrace nature, continue to ride, and most of all give Theresa some time to awaken to her spiritual energy.

Arriving home near supper time, KR prepared some chicken soup and an egg salad sandwich with a side of pickles. All chased with a glass of milk. An addiction of his that he loved. Relighting the fire and taking his seat in a second-generation rocking chair, KR savored a glass of Merlot.

As the birch crackled and popped, he continued to read some Ayn Rand. One of his favorite authors, she had developed a philosophical system she named Objectivism. A fine read for anyone who thinks outside the box. Concluding that man is not considered equal in the eyes of his counterparts, he finished off the chapter and retired for the evening, drifting off to sleep within the warmth of the feather tick.

NINE

PANDEMIC

A pandemic had circled the globe, which threw society into turmoil. With egos and attitudes, man tackled the invader with all his lunacy on the front line. While keeping greed at the forefront, a high percentage of businesses remained open and money was printed to appease the wealthy. Two weeks into the pandemic and the credit generations were broke. Governments running in the red suddenly offered money to anyone who could not feed themselves. The general public did not seem to be concerned and went about their daily programmed lives. A lot of them were working to keep the change in their pockets, while others were able to work from their homes, which kept their employers smiling as the greenbacks continued to roll in. Being frugal had been one of KR's fundamental life choices over the years and the frugality did come in handy at this time. He was convinced that man would never be able to structure a society without the implementation of greed. Sooner or later Capitalism would implode.

KR had not heard or seen Theresa since the outbreak started but knew she was well and kept his distance. Not knowing whether he was asymptomatic or not, he would not risk infecting her or anyone else for that matter. Not knowing when or if the Covid-19 pandemic would end, KR continued with his long-range plan of moving.

Keeping himself grounded to Mother Earth, KR focused on the future and immediate tasks to be completed. His plan was taking shape as if he were being guided in some way. Daily meditations continued and his life began to change little by little each day.

The fire pit was alight and the dried out poplar, cut the year before, popped and crackled. The logs burned fast and hot leaving a vast amount of coals. Not letting them go to waste, KR decided to roast up a couple of smokies. He garnished them with mustard and relish, and washed them down with, of course, a Classic. While indulging in the last smoky, his finely tuned ear picked up the chatter of solid lifters. As the sound became more apparent, Slim idled up the drive.

Slim dismounted the hard tail with a grim look and concern within his demeanor. KR stoked up the fire, passing an Innis to his visitor. Slim relayed the news that Wyatt had disappeared and had not been seen for several days. Supposedly returning from a sit down with a rival club, he had vanished from the grid, leaving worry and speculation amongst his club brothers. Slim was relieved to be free from the club life. Although KR was concerned for his old friend, he was not surprised and understood the seedy underworld of bike culture. KR and Slim would continue to ride as independents, blazing a trail in a new direction, leaving the clubs and the running shoe riders behind them. Only the wind would be at their backs. With the Innis finished, Slim entered the saddle, fired his ride and rode home. Leaving KR to absorb the information he had left.

With the energy of the full moon and the disappearance of Wyatt, KR knew he would not sleep well. Some meditation would be needed to enter the dream world.

KR had felt another card being drawn to be put into play. Intuition filled his sails, propelling him forward. Theresa's energy mixed with the wind was directing his path. All was well within the daydream. From the crow's nest a new reality was straight ahead. Through a light mist he saw a lych gate, with no gate keeper in sight. As the mist vanished, KR found himself alone by the fire, realizing that meditation or sleep was not always needed to enter the dream world.

This daydream was similar to his fire gazing experience at Calling Creek. The lifting of the veil was becoming easier for him, the visions clearer and more concise. They revealed more and more information pertaining to his journey. With some repetition, they explained a purpose still hidden, but emerging with every little detail hidden within the visions. He was becoming more aware of Theresa, who had become the main constant of his dreams, reading and visions. Always a participant in his new reality, KR found peace and solace as dawn broke each day. A psychologist may have diagnosed him as a borderline psychotic, but KR's journey was as right as rain.

Never being one to worry about what people thought of him, KR never paid any attention to those who could not relate.

The air chilled with the sinking of the sun and with the fire once again stoked, KR grounded himself to Mother Earth. With a smile he warmed himself as Theresa entered through the back door of his mind, closing it behind her, just like she had done so many times before.

The pandemic was showing signs of weakening in some parts of the world where populations were sparse and spread out over larger areas. KR lived amongst a population of fifty thousand, so infections and deaths had been minimal. Restrictions were about to be lifted and some sectors of the economy were to reopen. As this news surfaced among the public, tensions eased off and the rat race stepped on the gas pedal a wee bit. Intuition was knocking at the back door and KR planned a surprise visit to the big box store. Feeling a bit relieved and with the need for some live music, KR hoped the worst was over, even though it could be some time before the larger venues would be open again. He would continue using the collected analog equipment in his basement, spinning vinyl and playing tape. Music had never let him down and like Theresa it was always there when needed.

There is an old saying within the biker culture for those old enough to remember: "When a woman walks away looking back over her shoulder, go after her!" And KR had never forgotten those wise words. All that he was going through currently in his life emphasized the words so much more. Shining the light upon his path and impossible to stray from it, he persevered in hopes that Theresa's reflection would be seen in him.

As the sun dove beyond the horizon and the coals of the fire glowed no more, KR headed indoors to relax a while longer. Noticing a text message, he flipped open the phone.

Wolf? This was perplexing and unexpected. A return trip across the Acheron River was deemed impossible to the inhabitants of Landing. But the truth was reviled and Wolf was walking the streets once again. The ferryman had explained that payment paid after crossing one way would garner a return trip, and so it was.

He had spent seven days searching for what many people call Hades but it could not be found. There was no fire, no tortured souls, demons, or ghosts. Just a spirit guide entrusted to direct souls on their way home, who explained that Hades only existed within man's 3-D realm.

THE INTROVERTED REBEL

FOLLOWING THE PATH OF HIS HEART

IS CAST INTO SOCIETY'S SHADOW

LIVING FROM WITHIN

AND SHEDDING HIS EGO

HE PERSEVERES

-RBK

TEN

ALIGN AND SHIFT

Beaker had left a first-class video message on Skype. KR grinned and smiled as he watched and listened to the engine wizard. His wicked mustache twitched as he relayed eight words. "Cone knuckle finished. Pick up at your convenience." KR would leave in the morning before sunrise. Anticipation would be hard to control. Reserving a truck, the plan was activated. Dawn would come so ever slowly. KR enjoyed his own company and always had. The trip would be made solo giving him a chance to reflect, along with some road tunes and solitude. The silence within would be placed in his heart space.

He slept soundly through the night until the flip phone vibrated as the rising sun closed dawn's gateway. KR prepared while the truck warmed. Rainwright was the destination, a ninety-minute drive east. Traffic was light and he went full ahead.

He thought of two Latin words - intro (to the inside) and vertere (to turn). So introversion was to turn within to live a rich inner life. Yes, KR was an introvert, which gave him the tools for his journey – an inner insight that the extroverts wished they had.

As the drive continued, past relationships were remembered and how they had played out in the lower frequencies. Disaster was that end game. KR knew that the higher frequencies would deliver a lasting relationship, far superior in every way. Nothing on earth would compare, and KR knew without a doubt that the intuition within his heart space had led him home.

Arriving on Rainwright Main Street, he thought what a cool place - small and quite simple with content people going about their day. The introverted KR could totally relate.

Shooting the shit with Beaker as the motor was loaded was always informative. As they parted ways, KR's grin was from ear to ear. Westbound it was.

With the knuckle loaded securely, strapped in like a baby in a car seat, KR headed west. With road tunes playing and the sun shining, his intuition had been intense all day with the thought of visiting Theresa. Giving him the green light, he would proceed. The drive had tired him, and sleep was needed. He retired early and followed the sandman to the edge of the forest where Plasoveus only smiled as they walked toward the brook. The smile reassured KR that all would be well the next day.

Breakfast would consist of slow cooked rolled oats and raisins, topped with a sprinkle of brown sugar and milk. It would stick to his ribs and take him through the day. After adding some air to the front tire, he was ready to roll and headed to the retail store.

The pandemic was still placing some restrictions on the public and KR found himself waiting outside before entering. The store was a mad house and Theresa was way too busy for a conversation, which was understandable. He decided to inquire at human resources, thinking that they might be hiring. KR lined up an interview for the next day and headed home.

With the prospect of a possible rehire, KR was hopeful and welcomed the return of the familiar smile followed by Theresa's daily greeting. "Happy to see you." Feeling at peace for the first time in a long while, KR bathed in his contentment. Stopping on his way home in a secluded park, he sat and meditated, taking in the moment and the recent peace that had befallen him. That night's sleep was peaceful and undisturbed by any lower energies.

The interview was set for three in the afternoon. All was well and KR felt great and relaxed, anticipating a good result as he sat waiting. His interviewer just happened to be his previous boss. The interview went off without a hitch and he was informed that they would let him know soon. Exiting the interview room, he glanced over his left shoulder.

There she was, with that well-remembered smile from centuries gone past, bewitching KR for an instant. He sat with Theresa as she ate her lunch. Both at ease with each other, conversation between the two was nothing new. KR was at peace within her presence and dreamed of her smile reappearing more often than not.

The snowflake obsidian stone was used to expel and protect from negative energies. Bathing it under moonlight would enhance its effectiveness two-fold. Offering the stone to his friend, she graciously accepted it, warming KR's heart more than she was aware. He felt he could tell her anything and was not afraid to speak his truth. No matter what anyone thought, Theresa had awakened his soul, setting it free to experience higher frequencies.

With lunch concluded, they walked together, agreeing with one another that they had made each other's day. KR wanted to embrace her tightly but understood that Theresa's karmic relationship was still in play and KR would never invade that space. Only their souls understood their connection in the fifth dimension. A connection that Theresa was gradually becoming aware of and KR, being the more awakened twin, was fully aware of. Departing from one another, peace and tranquility filled his heart space.

KR woke with that peaceful feeling that had engulfed him the last couple of days, but it seemed to have dissipated somewhat. Intuition told him to make a follow up call regarding the interview, sensing that something was off. The conversation ended with "not at this time." As the call ended with the line still open, KR could hear two voices speaking: "Who was that on the phone?" "Just that guy we do not want to hire!" KR's heart hit the floor. At that precise moment, the vision of that well-remembered smile disappeared from his mind's eye, sending him into a tailspin like no other before.

KR had lived his whole life as an introverted rebel, segregated from mainstream society. Nothing surprised him and he realized that there was no intention to hire him. But all was not lost, he had spent an unforgettable moment in time with Theresa that would never be forgotten, and maybe one day it could be material for a book.

The following morning was brutal for KR. He felt as if the dark night had reappeared and it scared him so. He was teeter tottering in the space between sanity and insanity. To sleep was all he wanted, and meditation was needed. Not leaving the house all day, despair began to appear and stir his foundation at its core. Meditation was his salvation and grounded him back to his new reality as he realized that this trigger would not affect his divine connection with Theresa.

What had he learned from this experience? He did not know at this time, but the lesson would manifest itself when useful to him, enlightening his journey even further.

ELEVEN

DINNER-PARTY

REFLECTION

Having a few personal mottos in his life kept KR on track and true to his word, which was especially important to him. And straying away from materialism was a main objective. Now Harleys and collecting music were not deemed as materialistic in his view, more of an addiction he would say. Two addictions that had kept him sane for years. Knowing what he needed and what he did not makes all the difference in a man's materialistic ideals. Frugality played a major role in his life and many people that passed through his life could not relate, leaving him once again on the sidelines. Paying no attention, he went about his life, managing quite well and living within his own parameters of solitude until his fifty-ninth year, when Theresa made her entrance into his life.

Returning home from shopping one afternoon, while going through his mail, he came across an incredibly unique letter. It had a stamped seal initialed S.G holding it shut. As he broke the seal and withdrew the contents, he found a dinner party invitation, with special guest speaker Liz J Gardner.

Sylvia had outdone herself, proving that she was quite eccentric, something which KR never questioned. He would absolutely accept the invitation without hesitation. More information about the paranormal would be welcomed.

Liz had the credentials of psychic medium, divine channeler and spirit extractor. She hailed from Boston, Massachusetts and would be staying with Sylvia for the summer. She would be reading for clients throughout her stay. This intrigued KR and he could not wait for the dinner.

With the sound of the door knocker, the door swung open. As KR crossed the threshold, he was introduced and entered the land of the paranormal. Psychics and mediums mingled with people from all walks of life, while vintage wines and whiskeys were savored within the palates of the guests. It was like stepping back into history. The time period authenticity of the library was evocative to KR, enhancing a daydream that brought with it a silhouette observed from the corner of his eye. Indulging his palate with the last of his Merlot, he took his seat.

Liz J Gardner was not new to the paranormal field and was universally recognized for her abilities. She was second to none in her field with a well-documented history of helping others connect with loved ones on the other side, expel dark energies and entities, and help twin flames on their journeys to union. These were just a few of her gifts. Her energy could be felt within the room and radiated a warm sense of healing. She was the real deal and KR had to have her read for him.

Dinner was served and KR indulged: Roast beef and mashed potatoes smothered with homemade gravy with a side of baby carrots, followed by apple cobbler and a cup of black tea.

While mingling with the guests, he was introduced to Liz. Finding her a warm and gentle soul they conversed while savoring some brandy. Agreeing to read for KR, an appointment would be set up through e-mail.

With a pounding head from the devil's medicine, KR swallowed some aspirin and started his day. In high spirits, he felt rejuvenated in a way but also felt that his heart space was only half full. There was always another half needed to make him whole, and knowing who would fill it gave him peace as he popped some whole wheat into the toaster. Intense emotions would surface from time to time, but some breathing techniques seemed to be helping to ease and release them, transmuting them back into the universe. He had learnt through his information gathering that surfacing emotions were past life traumas being released. Dreams were also used for this purpose - a process of the spiritual path, cleansing the soul and expelling one's ego. Complete liberation of the soul from all its limiting factors in its past life experiences was the goal KR had set himself and he was determined to reach it. With the help of Theresa, the goal was attainable. She was the current beneath the galleon while he manned the crow's nest.

At this point in his journey KR found himself on the river of no return. It was too late to turn back with the junction in sight, and the lighted lantern growing brighter. The rudder was directing the way home and the starry night was exposing the lych gate, but the gate keeper was nowhere to be found.

As the computer booted up, some peace had returned to KR's heart space and the familiar energy engulfed him once again. Checking his e-mail, he found one new message: "Reading scheduled Monday May 18/20 6pm. Thx Liz."

This was great news - exactly one week away. The anticipation was remarkably high, and KR decided to add some more meditation to his days, converge with nature more regularly and directly in hopes that he could control and eventually eliminate any of the seven deadly sins he had acquired throughout his incarnations. They should be replaced with chastity, moderation, charity, diligence, patience, kindness and humility. Achieving this milestone would enhance his ascension tremendously.

Knowing and realizing that some profound changes had occurred within the last year drove him further inward and possibly searching for solitude once again. Although intuition was telling him to share his story and spread the word to all those who would listen contently. He would start to journal his journey for future reference.

KR had already been drawn to several awakened souls who did not shy away from the subject. Finding it refreshing, he began to seek out others who would converse on the subject material. Relinquishing his story gave him peace and purpose, solidifying his connection with Theresa.

With the advancement of summer just around the corner, KR found himself dipping into some mattress money and contemplated looking for work other than the retail store. But the remnants of the pandemic left the world with high unemployment and an unsure future for the blue-collar man. He was thankful for his frugality and thought of his grandfather for a moment. The generation that lived without credit, bought only what they needed and could afford, and within their smiles were happy each and every day.

Fourteen months into his journey, the path had been riddled with ups and downs, twists and turns, emotional lows and highs. Doubt and fear were mixed together stirring his emotions at any time, leaving KR to question his sanity. But the silhouette steering the galleon straight toward the light visible from the crow's nest made perfect sense. With the course laid out, together they were a team, in it until the end. The finish line would soon appear and together the journey would be completed.

Choosing the road less travelled would be called frivolous by many, but being different was a character trait that KR had embraced his entire life. He chose with his heart, letting it lead the entire way. Stumbling and falling he continued to get up.

TWELVE

GROUNDED & COMMITTED

Moisture from the heavens had turned the earth the color of green, ushering in new beginnings for KR. Not knowing when he would see Theresa again, he withdrew deeper within. Concentrating on the build and the California trip, de-cluttering his home and preparing for his move to Trail, he imagined her by his side. Knowing that each of them had their own spiritual work to complete and understanding the universe was in complete control, guiding them both to union.

The painted picture that KR had placed within his mind's eye was starting to materialize as the summer approached - he would stay close to home and commence his long-range goal. Keeping his commitment to his journey and purpose, time was irrelevant and his team from the angelic realms was never out of reach.

Trying to stay grounded in the moment, KR fired the pan and hit the road. The cool wind blew his ponytail from side to side. The foliage emerging from its winter hibernation left a lingering scent of a future summer. As the road twisted and turned, Green Grass Cemetery came into view and the pan eventually came to rest in front of the gate. Turning the key, the pan was silenced.

As he entered through the gate, stillness and serenity took center stage alongside peacefulness. Allowing KR to ground himself within that exact moment. Theresa filled his heart space and he was content in that moment. Savoring the experience, he meditated with the breeze. Seeing her the week before seemed like an eternity ago.

That evening brought with it the smell of smoke and old school Harleys. With old friends gathered around the fire pit, the crackling birch burned slowly. All riders for the California trip were in attendance, there was Innis in a tub of ice and smokies being roasted. The trip was still a year ahead and preparations continued. Slim would be asked to tag along - all were in favor.

With the last rumble, his guests had vacated his back yard and KR stoked the fire in preparation for some fire gazing. He was accustomed to it and was finding it easy to access his visions.

As he gazed into the fire, his eyes focused on the flames, directing his sight toward the coals. Reds, blues, yellows, orange and a deep crimson right near the bottom raised the veil behind his eyes revealing a road sign: Shelter Bay 2 kilometers. To his right Theresa was sitting beside him. As the veil appeared the vision vanished from his eyes and feeling a chill from the late-night air, KR entered his home.

Now Shelter Bay was south of Revelstoke - a landing for the ferry that crossed upper Arrow Lake - a beautiful spot that KR had visited several times throughout his life. A few days prior to the fire gazing vision, the same vision had appeared to KR out of the blue in the middle of the day with the words "I've got to show you something."

Becoming more accustomed and in tune with his newfound gifts and senses, he let the universe take the reins.

Slim was en route and KR prepared for a ride. The more he rode, the more grounded he felt. As Slim rolled in, KR had the pan running and off they went. Riding the secondaries where traffic was sparse, the rhythm of the V-twins was in unison and the air around them engulfed them in their own realities. No one could enter and time was nonexistent. KR relished this time and space with the wind at their backs. The straight pipes barked and growled as the speed increased.

They pulled into Alberta Sands, a small hamlet near the edge of a lake. With a kick ass dinner they let the hard tails cool while they ingested some saturated fat. Slim placed the order: "Fries and gravy and a Classic. Double it."

The two of them both being introverts and rebels were used to being ostracized by society. They enjoyed each other's company and smiled as all eyes followed them to their seats. Riding old school chops did gather some attention and that was the whole point. To be different!

California drifted into their conversation. Slim was curious about how the planning was evolving and KR took it upon himself to ask Slim if he would be interested in coming along. Slim's eyes lit up like a Christmas tree and without hesitation he accepted. That would be five in total. All were seasoned riders who could ride hard when needed and understood that danger could exist around any corner.

The return trip brought with it the anticipation of his reading with Liz. It was two days away and KR was nervous and excited. His guidance had led him all the way this far and nothing could detour him now.

For years deep thought had become second nature to KR and he began to evaluate and question man's sexual energy. Sex is the center of all life and creation. The energetic core of life and man's sexual energy was the doorway to his creativity, joy and deep spiritual growth. Sexual transmutation when practiced would channel and direct the energy into a higher purpose.

Sex within in our 3-D realm did not entice KR any longer, with all its negativity and the conditions placed upon it. Contemplating a venture into the ancient world of tantric edging, he was hopeful that abstinence could be achieved, preparing him for the 5-D experience, which surpassed any man's conception of sex.

The instant thoughts and visions were becoming more frequent and seemed to be glimpses into the future. Simple and precise, they always made KR hopeful, guiding him with direction and clarity. Whenever he needed some reassurance on his journey they would appear.

One late afternoon while meditating in a secluded park, the sun was warming his face while the breeze whispered through the trees. A vision passed before his eyes, leaving a painted picture to observe and he felt his heart space filled once again.

Billowy clouds floated above within the pacific blue sky. A slight breeze tousled their hair as they both smiled, arms around each other. A picture was taken and the emotion of the vision was felt intensely within that instant.

His transformation continued daily, which he embraced as he continued to adapt and integrate all that was received. Climbing the ladder one rung at a time, ascension reminded him each day of its rigors and obstacles. The small circle of friends and family surely would not understand. Feeling no need to explain, KR kept it to himself. After all it was all for Theresa.

And yet again he loved her another day more than the day before.

Like the disappearing ripples upon the water, daybreak introduced a new day and the reading with Liz was scheduled for 6pm MST. KR would spend the day replacing a front-end tube seal on the pan, which would hamper the anticipation of the reading a bit. Looking forward to some validation from his spiritual team and conversing with Theresa's higher self would give him direction on how to proceed.

THIRTEEN

READING

The sound of the door knocker was answered with a hug followed by Sylvia's warm smile. Inviting KR into the library, Liz was all prepared to read. Crystals of all shapes and sizes were placed on the table with two lit candles - one blue, one green. Dressed in the style of a spiritual psychic of the forties, the atmosphere within the library was unique to say the least. Taking his seat as Sylvia left the room, they were about to begin. Commencing with a grounding prayer and protection, angels, guides and ascended masters were called forth.

Celtic druids and sages from Ireland provided the first words relayed from the spirit realm. KR was an advanced sensitive old soul completing his last incarnation. Being a druid himself from previous incarnations, he had the ability to communicate with trees, spirit elements and animals. He was an empath who could feel emotional energy and messages from the spiritual realms. Hearing and speaking to the angels were other gifts that were manifesting.

KR had noticed two crows sitting in a tree while out for a walk one afternoon. Feeling their energy, he observed them for a short time before they flew off. Crows are the keepers of karmic law, helping him end karmic cycles of fear, connect to the spirit world, balance and transform. He had entered the crossroads where healing and transformation were about to take place.

The heritage of Celtic Ireland was embedded in his soul along with the wisdom and spirituality of the druids and tree sages. He was guided to inspire all who would listen and stepped into the role of spiritual teacher, spreading the word of the realms upon the earth and enlightening the awakened.

Changing subjects to the divine feminine - yes, there was absolutely a twin flame involved. The other half of KR's soul - Theresa! This was another validation, but KR had felt in his heart space for quite some time that their connection was divine. There was a lot more information pertaining to both that did solidify their connection and which would be kept between all three parties for now. Lots of information pertaining to Theresa was revealed that clarified that she had entered a crossroads as well. Healing and preparing for transformation, union would manifest with divine timing.

The realm guided his planned move to Trail - connecting to spiritual people and his new surroundings would bring him peace and contentment, enhance his gifts and move him closer to the 5-D. He was also guided to establish a YouTube channel - he would enlighten the masses as the dawn of Aquarius ushered in the golden era.

Shamanism was also mentioned, and KR was to dig deeper into the ancient realm. Something he would follow up with enthusiasm. Having the thought shoot through his mind days before the reading was no coincidence.

Clear guidance was affirmed through the information obtained from the reading. Liz was one of a kind and delivered an exceptional reading. No stone was left unturned with questions asked and answered. Theresa and KR's joint mission had been sealed the day one soul was spilt in two.

Liz would be asked to read in the future when guided by source.

Two days after the reading, KR was restless. Peace began to saunter into his heart space, filling it gently. The restlessness disappeared as Theresa's energy filled the last half, rendering KR into a new state of consciousness.

The incline of his path had lessened to a degree with the odd stone causing him to stumble from time to time. Regaining his footing, he focused on the outcome and forged ahead. Adding all that he had learnt to the arsenal of his ascension tactics, every piece of information attained from the reading was absorbed.

Four days after the reading another crow appeared, clearing karmic cycles, closing opened doors and ushering in KR's transformation. Seeing the crow excited him and gave him strength and optimism for the future. Thoughts and visions were becoming commonplace and all had been journaled for some future purpose he was not yet aware of.

Looking back at his earlier life, KR was known in certain circles as Tall. It was a part of his life that had dissipated like a heavy fog vanishing from sight, never again entering his vision. A forgotten world lived within lower energies and frequencies, locking him into a state of confusion and chaos. Leading a life of uncertainty with no direction, he tripped stumbled and fell often. Picking himself up after every occurrence he never really stayed on track until Theresa entered his life, steering the galleon from the stern.

Now direction had been established with the sun rising each day and lighting the way like the silhouette at the entrance to the bridge. What was to be found on the other side was unknown, but hand in hand Theresa and KR would walk across together.

FOURTEEN

RUN

Northern Alberta, with its sparse populations and miles of open road with long gentle curves, was ideal for riding at high speeds. Assiniboine was a little village hidden within a forest of spruce trees, some so large that a pair of hands could not encircle them. Standing eighty feet tall, their beauty was breath taking. It was an untouched part of the world that man had not yet destroyed and KR loved the area.

This would be the first ride that the five would ride together. Preparing for the California trip, it would sync them together as a team. KR and Ramrod would take lead riding side by side, followed by Lurch and Psycho, with Slim taking up the rear and keeping an eye on the bikes as they rode. Leapfrogging when passing vehicles, everyone synced well together. After all they had been riding for years and had acquired years of experience between them all.

Pulling into a small campground on the outskirts of Assiniboine, they lit a small fire and enjoyed an old-fashioned picnic and some community. This would be an introduction to what the trip would entail and all the posse were ecstatic.

It was late afternoon and with the bikes warmed, they saddled up and headed home. Wyatt was still missing, and KR reflected on his old friend as the sun sank lower beneath the treetops. His riding companions noticed the changes occurring within KR and accepted him with respect, listening to him contently as he began to speak his newfound truth more often. He had a sense of clarity of where his path was leading him.

A vote had been taken at the campground and the consensus was that one more rider was to be found for the trip, making three pairs of riders. An even number of riders is more unique than an odd number, but finding another rider would not be easy. Just the simple fact that build, ride and service your own had disappeared from the culture and those who did were few and far between. The riders hanging on to the old school traditions were absolute diehards, keeping to themselves and having no concern whatsoever with the evolving running shoe riders. KR understood that new school would eventually become old school, with original traditions and culture lost in the tide of the past and never to return. Just like himself, the new had washed away the old, never to return.

It had turned out to be a great day and KR took solace in the solitude of his evening. With a cup of goat weed tea steeping beside his lazy boy, he opened chapter one of Shamanism For Beginners. Digging deeper into the ancient world of his past incarnations and wanting to unlock anything hidden within his soul, which would lead to living the rest of his days in a shamanic reality.

Channeling through Liz, KR's divine team clarified his journey with Theresa. A joint mission was to unfold together. The team described the junction, visions and dreams; provided guidance on syncs and signs, crows, numbers, and intuition. The list could go on and on. There was absolutely no doubt! The path was clear and his soul was in complete control now. The universe was guiding Theresa as she steered the galleon mid-river.

Only the awakened would understand. Twins incarnated at this time would be his allies and for those who would question his sanity, so be it! Hoping to help the newly awakened and those searching for answers, he contemplated ideas of information exchange.

FIFTEEN

NOTICEABLE CHANGES &
TRANSFORMATIONS

Being out among the public was starting to take its toll on KR. Feeling society's energies and the lower frequencies of the 3-D realm drained him of his energy and he needed to recharge after an outing. His growing empathic abilities also took a toll. Sensing people's frequencies was commonplace to him now and the lower ones raised havoc with his physical being, causing him to sleep ten plus hours a day and at times take a cat nap in the afternoon. Ascending from the lower frequencies to the higher frequencies was also a challenge. Knowing all would be well, he persevered, often asking himself the question: How many people have been awakened in the world?

The seven deadly sins! Man's learning list that he does not pay much attention to while living in the 3-D realm with the ego running the show, until that one fated day when the soul is called to awaken and the battle begins. KR totally understood this battle and his battles were victories now as the seven deadly sins were replaced with humility, kindness, patience, diligence, charity, moderation and chastity.

Looking back at the last fourteen months. The ups and downs on his rollercoaster ride had leveled out. The extreme emotional swings had calmed and the direction was known. With the union and a joint mission confirmed, KR could feel a transformation within the atmosphere. It gathered momentum as it glided toward the earth. Knowing its destination and recipient - the shaman would be reborn, breaking free from his imprisonment.

KR turned out the light, shutting his eyes to meet the sandman once again.

A passing thunderstorm crashed outside and awoke KR from his slumber. Starting his day with the thought of old times, for an instant he remembered the long-forgotten life of Tall, while realizing also that his KR persona would soon be lost in the past. They would be little more than footnotes left to deteriorate in a book not worth reading. Both parts of him that taught lessons learned and lived. Casting them aside, he welcomed the transformation to come.

Self-mastery was the objective now - to merge the higher frequencies with the lower frequencies while in human form. With the ego completely obliterated and having control of the lower energies, his soul would soar. Powered by the consciousness of the heart and fueled by unconditional love, to be his authentic self, KR once again welcomed the transformation with open arms.

On tenterhooks daily, his planned move grew closer as each day passed him by and being anxious was by no means a description of how he felt about the move. No words could explain it. It was a guided calling, which KR acknowledged and accepted as fate.

The gathering clouds slowed, and the rain steadied. The back door would not be opened. KR would indulge in one of God's greatest gifts of solitude. He would spend the day with his new literary friend: Shamanism For Beginners.

Rumor had it that Vincent Van Gogh was on a twin flame journey and it had driven him mad. KR could totally relate to the great painter's dilemma. There were times when he himself felt the world close in on him but the connection with Theresa always grounded him, strengthening his fate.

Peering out of his newly installed kitchen window, KR could see no sun, just heavy rain exploding as it hit Mother Earth. It disappeared into her dry soil and provided sustenance for the green that would surely appear within the foliage of summer. He daydreamed of memories past. Smiling as he prepared some breakfast while continuing to read his new literary friend.

KR found himself in a new comfort zone. Feeling grounded and more centered than ever before he continued to read. Absorbing this new information that felt so familiar to him stirred an old awareness reminiscent of days past. He was consumed and enlightened.

Turning the page, another chapter was finished and KR's thoughts drifted back to a morning not so long ago. Awakened from a deep sleep, he saw a vision so clear and vivid, like a road sign right in front of his eyes. "I miss you!" This had not been the first time this message had been relayed to him. Previously it had been audio. Knowing intuitively where these two messages came from, KR continued with his day, feeling the intensity of his and Theresa's connection growing daily and their telepathic abilities improving rapidly. This newfound sense of peace and stability within his life leveled out the path on which he travelled, and at times throughout the day it even seemed downhill.

Crows and ravens were frequent visitors while visiting nature. They were a reminder of his reading with Liz. Their part being played in his transformation was vital. Recently, visiting a graveyard for some solitude, an owl flew slowly into his view. Taking its perch within a large spruce tree, it took a rest from Mother Wind. It peered at KR for an instant. It was a guardian of wisdom, distributing to all at the crossroads of transformation.

Eclipses and full moon energies deliver shifts to humanity and Mother Earth, and KR found himself moon gazing and bathing in its light. Soaking up its energies while hoping to shift his own energy and transform further. Being at the crossroads of transformation was a pivotal point, teeter tottering him and readying to launch him further toward the lighted lantern. The ravens, the crows and the owl - their piercing eyes focused upon his soul. Remnants of the long-lost shaman emerged from the shadows of long forgotten incarnations, while the silhouette holding the lighted lantern stood just beyond the lych gate.

The KR persona was vanishing, stepping aside and making way for his true self.

SIXTEEN

EDUCATION OF THE SHAMAN

St. Peter's cemetery was close to his home and KR would visit frequently, keeping him grounded. The small cemetery with spruce and pine trees was well maintained and a distance from the main highway. The solitude amongst nature quieted his mind chatter. Absorbing the silence within its gates, the cemetery was his refuge, taking the edge off his transformation as he waited at the crossroads. Not knowing when the next shift would propel him forward, he spent his days within, devouring his new literary friend, turning page after page and absorbing all that was new and familiar. Shamanism had passed through his mind before the reading with Liz and the confirmation from his team to dig deeper intrigued KR.

Shamanism had been around for thirty thousand years, dating back to when our ancestors were still hunters and gatherers, living in harmony with Mother Earth and tending to her needs, while receiving all that was needed for an abundant existence. But modern technologies changed all that and with the domestication of animals and the invention of agriculture, man was no longer a hunter and gatherer, and the shamanic way of life began to disappear.

Religions sought to discredit the beliefs of the shaman, labeling their teachings as lies from the pits of hell. As technology advanced, further alienating people from nature, they disregarded all respect for nature and man was set on a path of destruction. Letting his greed lead the way, Mother Earth was left undefended. Shamanism was not a religion but a belief system.

There was a lot to learn and as KR continued to read he began to understand that the similarities between shamanism and his spiritual awakening were intertwined together. He understood that his emerging gifts could be used to facilitate a shamanic way of life and he would continue his quest.

Shamanism was unique in the way of its teachings, intertwining the spirit world with Mother Earth. Knowing that man was part of nature, the shaman held great respect for Mother Earth and treated her with dignity. A give and take scenario had evolved and a balance between Mother Earth and man was constant, until man's ego introduced him to greed! KR understood this all too well.

Experimenting with different states of consciousness is where he would start. These different states would include relaxation, focused attention, breath work, drumming and five others would be considered. Fasting was considered a purification ritual. Pushing one's limits could trigger an altered state of mind and allow spiritual light to enter their body.

Being familiar with fasting, KR decided to test his limits, and started off with a twenty-four hour fast. KR was tested and passed with flying colors. Drinking only clear liquids within that time period, he felt great and had more energy than ever before. Deciding to test himself further, he would start a regimen of daily fasting. Twenty-four, 20 – 20 – 20 – 20 – 20 – 20. Eating only once a day, the first week passed him by with no problems. He went through each day and was cool, calm and collected. His stomach even started to feel different, in a much better way. Liking the results, he decided to incorporate fasting into his way of life.

Visualization techniques would also be incorporated within his days. Five exercises would be experimented with. Picturing things in one's mind and exercising the imagination were a must for any novice shaman.

In order to perceive the worlds in which the spirits live, one must nurture one's five psychic senses first.

Paying more attention to the world around you and not letting anything escape your focus will strengthen your five senses and awaken the sixth.

Consciousness can be applied to three levels in psychic advancement. The conscious and subconscious mind followed by the super subconscious mind. Receiving messages from each other to keep you sane, more wise and powerful is the super subconscious mind. The universal mind, as it is considered, is where spiritual wisdom comes from. Along with your instincts, insights and psychic abilities, the subconscious serves as a gateway to the super subconscious. Considered to be the collective consciousness, where the Akashic Records are stored and available for one's personal download.

A shaman's power is not his to claim. Acting only as a hollow bone, so to speak, allowing the powers of spirit to enter and manifest in our reality. Therefore, being empty is crucial for an effective shaman and the main factor in being empty is the eradication of the ego. The hollower and emptier you become, the more authentic your experiences will become.

The lower world, middle world and upper world are all connected to each other and equal to one another, forming the mythological world tree believed within most cultures.

The lower world is a world of nature and the elements of the earth. Water, fire, air, earth, animal and plant life. Within this world wisdom can be gained from the animal and plant spirits. Their qualities can be bestowed upon the visiting shaman. Many things can be learnt in this world corresponding with the subconscious mind. The lower world deals with deep emotions, instincts, and habits, along with dreams. It's an earthly and natural environment like a forest or jungle where the inhabitants may appear to belong to indigenous tribes. Modern technology does not exist and plenty of animals roam free.

The middle world is the most chaotic of the three. It is where we use ordinary consciousness in a non-physical dimension of the world we live in. Our waking reality is located in the middle world and is a counterpart to our physical reality. Like our world in many ways, shamans travel to this world seeking answers for those living in the 3-D realm.

The upper world or Heaven as many call it, is where deities and angels can be found. It's a realm of spirit guides, ascended masters, saints, planetary beings and dwellers of the universe. The blueprint and potential that guides how reality manifests itself is controlled from the upper world, and it is said to be a shadow of what exists in our physical plane.

These three worlds fascinated KR and he would start to experiment with travelling to these worlds, seeking answers to his questions and the help needed for his own journey. Using shamanic drum music, he would first try entering the lower world in search of help with one of the seven deadly sins that had been pestering him all his life. The only one of the seven that hung on like a ball and chain, following him everywhere, a relentless adversary and a direct ally with his ego. Both needed to be eradicated for good.

June 21/20 Father's Day. KR awoke with a sense of displacement from society. The feeling had stirred him inside before, appearing every now and again to remind him once again that ascension was never easy and persistence was the key to victory. Consciousness happened in shifts and time was needed as one's transformation advanced.

The crossroad was a desolate place. He waited alone for a shift to move him forward toward the once dim lantern that grew brighter with every day that passed him by. He knew that the lantern bearer was waiting at her crossroad as well, diligently tending the lantern as its light continued to brighten.

Cycling was something that KR enjoyed all his life and he had incorporated it into his lifestyle. Everything was accomplished that needed to be done - groceries, errands etc. It was also a means of transportation within the city where he lived. Not driving for years, he accepted the lifestyle change as a part of his personal deprogramming.

He knew the city well and was accustomed to its trails and parks. He made enjoyable rides within the serenity of the small city and having found some quiet locations, he would meditate with nature, feeling the wind against his face, listening to Mother Wind blowing through the leaves of the trees and smelling the rain as it hit the earth beneath his feet. Merging with Mother Earth and feeling connected, he knew that all was intertwined with the universe.

As the pages continued to flip, the shaman within began to stir and awaken. Ideas exited his subconscious mind and entered his new consciousness, leaving him in wonderment at all that had transpired since meeting Theresa.

The space between sleep and being awake is where the shaman needs to enter in order to travel within the three worlds, and KR had entered this space for brief periods while meditating. He would experiment more and hone this exercise.

The world of the shaman was vast. Teachings and lessons for now would be self-taught but KR's wish for an apprenticeship would have to wait for the time being. Staying grounded in the 3-D world was of major importance. To anyone on the spiritual path and partaking with Mother Nature, footwear was the go-to tool for personal grounding. Wearing footwear such as moccasins or grounding straps attached to any kind of footwear would ground anyone directly to Mother Earth.

As the pages continued to flip, the last chapter was drawing near and the subject material within the remaining pages captivated the spellbound KR. Finishing his introduction to Shamanism, he decided to read it again and absorb what he may have missed. More material on the subject would have to be discovered and researched. The learning curve had begun and the shaman would emerge when the time was right. Perhaps his new surroundings in Trail would awaken the shaman hidden within his soul.

Transformation was not easy and finding one's true self was one hell of a ride. The battle between his soul and ego was constant but confirmation within his heart told him that his soul had the upper edge and not to lose hope. The lantern light only grew brighter and Theresa would meet him at the junction in due time.

Ups and downs, lows and highs, emotional triggers of any kind were all added into the mix, setting the stage for transformation and KR felt great most of the time. Feeling the odd low, he was holding his ground and moving toward his authentic self. He had made great strides within the last year and a change had come. With his shifting consciousness propelling him even further, persistence and time were on his side.

The summer solstice of 2020 was ushered in by a full moon. Followed by a new moon along with an eclipse, bringing change and new beginnings, and transmuting karma back into the universe. Feeling more authentic than ever before, KR started to flow with the universe. The future was clear – the galleon's sails were full once again.

A light drizzle had brought with it a moment in time that KR reflected on as he drank a cup of tea. Sitting in his lazy boy, the profound experience did not fade into oblivion. Captivating his thoughts, it lingered and was embedded in his conscious mind. Leaving him with even more clarity pertaining to his connection with Theresa, this experience had transpired before but the intensity of it was never as strong.

In the conscious state between wakefulness and sleep where one drifts in and out of sleep, KR felt their higher selves merge together. Two halves of the same soul reuniting in 5-D. Knowing exactly what was taking place, he drifted off into a peaceful sleep alongside his beloved. Their connection was growing intensely stronger just like the lantern's light, directing his way home.

The recent full moon lured KR to bathe in its light and soak up its energies, which travelled toward the earth. It was as though the man in the moon had called his name. Accepting the invitation, he felt the energies transform him further toward his authentic self. The memories of KR and Tall were becoming remnants of his past, soon to disappear like a snowflake hitting hot tinder. Transformation at the crossroads once again reminded KR of the desolation he felt.

Ever since he had taken up residence at the crossroads, waiting for his transformation, he had been sleeping on the side of his bed every night. The continued energy that Theresa sent his way was adding strength to his battle within and confronting the battle of the relentless sin allied with his ego. They would be abolished and transmuted back into the universe, never again to block his journey home.

SEVENTEEN

LURCH'S ACRE

The basement contained the dark no matter how bright the sun shone within the sky. Waking from a peaceful sleep, KR could smell the warmth of a beautiful day and began his day with some music. Helix, played loud of course. Old School was the title of their newest release, containing a single titled - "Closer", which he just loved. It reminded him of his most anticipated goal - to get closer to Theresa. The day had been designated for a ride to visit Lurch and some fire gazing was on the agenda.

It was after supper. The pan was fired and KR headed west. An hour's ride and he would arrive at his destination. The sun was sinking on the horizon and a light breeze rippled the treetops as the pan growled through the twists and turns of the secondary highway. With not a car in sight, he would arrive in good time.

Two gargoyles guarded the entrance on each side. Lurch was found stoking the fire as KR brought the pan to a halt. Embracing in a bear hug, KR and Lurch commenced their conversation where the previous one ended. Both enjoying each other's company, they listened to each other without judgment and never criticized or questioned the other's beliefs. Soul mates through and through, they had lived many incarnations together and KR was grateful that he could share his spiritual awakening and all its details with him.

As the sun dropped below the treetops, KR warmed himself beside the fire and enjoyed the peace that had become his closest friend. Seemingly hanging around more often, he accepted its presence with his stay at the crossroads of transformation, while he waited patiently for another shift in his consciousness.

The concrete jungle was left behind in the rearview mirror of the pan and in that moment, while warming by the fire, KR felt the ease and grace of the universe as he was guided further along his path. With every shift in consciousness and every moment of reality on the other side of the veil, wandering away from the 3-D constructs in which we all live was becoming easier. His life had changed drastically and it felt good!

Conversation was never an issue between the two soul mates, but neither was silence. Silence was always the threshold of conversation and Lurch and KR were masters of each. The mix of birch and spruce burned rapidly together, while the sparks lit up the night sky as a new moon began to rise, sending its energies toward all who would accept. The flames rose with intensity, with the colors of orange and white reflecting off surrounding poplar trees. The embers were beginning to call out and the shaman within KR became anxious. As the flames tapered softly the embers called once again.

The stage had been set. The colorful embers were a mix of crimson in the center and were changing color as they cooled: reds, blues, yellow and orange dancing within the eyes of the spectators. KR found himself once again in familiar surroundings - the edge of the forest where he had been led before. The newly awakened shaman confirmed this was the lower world. His spirit guide Plasoveus was waiting for him. Acknowledging each other, they proceeded toward the brook. Coming upon the brook where the water had slowed, a small pool of water was reflecting like a mirror and reflected an image not forgotten by KR.

A pair of eyes was staring back at him, so familiar and reminiscent, they danced with the slight ripples upon the water, never leaving his gaze. As a tear splashed the surface, the frequent silhouette appeared, holding the lighted lantern and with a faint whisper as she disappeared. "I'll see you soon."

Plasoveus led the way, following the familiar path traveled before, it was overgrown with lush green vegetation. They slowly made their way toward the entrance and the ladder that would take KR to the middle world. Glancing back as he ascended the ladder, he saw that Plasoveus had vanished, leaving KR to journey alone.

The lych gate was engulfed within the gate keeper's shadow. As he approached, the gate keeper started to speak and the recognizable voice took KR by surprise. A message has been left for you said the gatekeeper. The three-word message "WAIT FOR ME" has been delivered. Shaken and disoriented for an instant, KR then abruptly found himself beside the fire, shaken and stirred once again. Lurch attended to the fire as they enjoyed the silence within.

KR now understood that the awakening shaman within and his spiritual gifts were intertwined, and were to be incorporated together as one.

The pristine conditions were ideal for a night ride home. It would give KR time to evaluate his journey to the lower and middle worlds, and to sort out any messages and their meanings that would apply to his twin flame journey.

As he let out the clutch, KR headed north and then east the rest of the way home. The melodic rhythm of the motor cleared his mind chatter. The voice of the gate keeper belonged to Wyatt, his old friend that was last seen aboard the ferry crossing the Acheron River.

The eyes staring back at him no doubt belonged to Theresa. He had never forgotten that day in the lunchroom at the big box store. Hugging each other while peering down into her eyes. Reflecting the recognition and validation of their spiritual connection, both knew on a soul level and KR also realized their connection in the 3-D realm. Feeling their energies merge, he did not want to let go of her.

It seemed like oh so long ago, and ever since that day she had become part of him. Completing him in every way possible, she was the catalyst to his awakening, they were the yin and yang to each other. KR being the awakened twin had no idea at the time where his path would lead him. Two halves of the same soul had merged, their soul contracts were initiated and their spiritual ascensions had begun. Their joint mission together would be the finale - to anchor their light in Trail as the realms guided their future.

KR idled up the drive, content with the peace within. Being guided to write a book, he would follow the guidance and began to write.

As he sat down and began to type, a song flashed through his mind - a timeless classic written by Ken Hensley and Lee Kerslake of Uriah Heep. "Come back to me" - a beautiful ballad that once again brought a tear to his eye. Contemplating the relevance of the ballad, page one had entered history.

EPILOGUE

Sixteen months had passed since meeting Theresa and the world KR now lived in was drastically different from the previous one. He now found himself at the crossroads, transforming into his authentic self, one day at a time. Waiting for another shift in consciousness, he would hold space while waiting for her.

Their previous separation at the junction had given them different paths to follow. Healing their souls as they traveled back to the crossroads, KR arrived first and would wait for the lighted lantern to appear, hearing her words echo once again within the whispering wind. "I'll see you soon."

FRIEND

MY DEAR OLD FRIEND

TIME HAS ELUDED US

UNTIL NOW

REUNITED AGAIN

ONE LAST INCARNATION TOGETHER

STEP INTO THE LIGHT

COME FIND ME

I AM WAITING FOR YOU

COME BACK TO ME

THERESA

-RBK

MY LIFE

MY STORY

MY JOURNEY

A LOVE STORY

BOOK THREE

IN PRESENT TENSE

-RBK

AN

R

B

K

READ

PROLOGUE

At this point in my journey, I was all in and dedicated to the evolution of my soul. Following it and hanging on while I held space for Theresa to have a shift in consciousness and acknowledge our spiritual connection. My love for her grew intensely as each day passed. It was unconditional of course, with compromise not being included in the love we shared in the 5-D realm. My non-fiction story continues as I prepared my move to Trail while navigating the twin flame journey laid out before me.

ONCE YOU AWAKEN

YOU WILL HAVE NO INTEREST

IN JUDGING THOSE WHO SLEEP

-UNKNOWN

Part Three

MY PILGRIMAGE CONTINUES

ONE

PRESENT TENSE

Shirley MacLaine, an awakened front-runner to the dawning of man's spiritual evolution, stood her ground amidst the controversy of her book Out on A Limb. Grounding herself in her authentic truth, she weathered out the storm and led the charge to the awareness of man's spirituality that had been dormant within mainstream society. Breaking the barriers and revealing hidden truths, she has paved the way for the awakened to follow her example and I tip my hat to her for her perseverance, strength and courage.

My calendar was flipped to August 2020 and I wondered where the time had gone. It felt just like yesterday that I had walked through those sliding doors at the retail outlet, having no concept of what would transpire. I now found myself out on a limb. Walking forward, I placed one foot in front of the other, one at a time like a tightrope walker. Never looking back, I hoped that the limb would hold as I travelled further along its length. My love for Theresa was intensifying with each day that passed and with my sights set on manifested union in the 3-D physical realm, I continued my journey.

The first installment of my book had been published and I was extremely excited to hold a hardcover in my hands. The sense of completion was overwhelming - I had followed through with my mission and was delighted with the final product.

Tuesday August 4/20 - this was the day. My heart's intuition had led my soul to the retail outlet. Within my hands I held a signed hardcover. The only one I would ever sign. I personally delivered it to Theresa with my heart pounding in anticipation of her reaction.

Her excitement brought with it her wonderful smile that stopped me dead in my tracks as my heart skipped a beat. Once again there was that familiar light in her eyes, recognizing our spiritual connection on a soul level.

It was so good to see her and that feeling reminiscent of long ago strengthened the familiar sense of home. Feeling at ease and comfortable, our conversation was continued from where the last one ended. It was some time ago but felt like yesterday.

Being the awakened twin, I lived with the constant knowing of our spiritual connection and by this time in my journey, I was so far out on the limb there was absolutely no turning back. The lighted lantern was still firmly in my sights.

My ascension was leading me to the fifth dimension while living in the third and I was beginning to understand the separation of the two. Being aware was giving me clarity about the density consciousness we are all born into.

The density consciousness was keeping Theresa mired in the 3–D physical realm. A quagmire of mixed emotions and a karmic partner were keeping her from walking the limb with me, and I knew that reading my book would awaken her to our connection. But when? After all it was my angels and guides who directed me to pass the book on to her, explaining that the book would trigger her awakening. But I asked myself once again: But when?

The mornings were getting cool and the leaves on the trees took on rainbow colors. I had just flipped the calendar again and September slumbered in. With twenty 20 nearing its end, I focused my efforts on house renovations.

Never looking back, I continued my high wire walk. The limb grew longer and longer as I progressed. Always knowing that the universe had my back, with destiny and fate at the forefront, my soul followed the intuition of my heart. The limb was securely anchored at the trunk and my new home in Trail was set in my sights.

It had been nineteen months since I first walked through those sliding doors at the retail store. Like stepping into another dimension, I navigated all the roadblocks and obstacles in my way, grew accustomed to all the ups and downs, lows and highs and adjusted to all the emotional swings that surfaced from the depths of my soul. Learning and soaking up as much spiritual information as I could, I became adept and informed on the twin flame phenomenon. I embraced my newly found authentic self and waited for transformation and another shift in my consciousness. But at this point in my journey I started to ask a recurring and valid question: when will Theresa awaken to our spiritual connection? Maybe I should not be asking this question, but of late it seemed to have invaded my thoughts and without a doubt it needed to be answered. I knew patience was key.

Being the first awakened twin and realizing our connection, I was the chaser, overstepping Theresa's boundaries at times but with respect and unconditional love at the forefront of our friendship of course. I became tired and disillusioned. The chase was not fruitful and I decided to let go and surrender as much as I could. I knew this would be hard and once again patience was key. The universe had my back and the limb was strong and sturdy at the trunk.

Moving forward with my new intention, I initiated the surrender phase. Not really knowing whether my decision was conscious or not, or maybe just a point in my journey - predestined perhaps? I felt I needed to try and a sense of running was soon replaced by peacefulness - until September 7th/20.

Throughout my journey I had learned to live with Theresa's all-so-frequent energy merging with my aura at any time. While out and about fulfilling some errands I was engulfed by her energy, so strong and intense that I had to take a breath and relax. Overwhelming with an intensity never felt before, it was another confirmation of our connection, which in hindsight my intuition has always known.

Unrequited love is a scenario that happens frequently within our society and is snickered at by the observers, especially when there is a karmic partner involved. For those living in the density consciousness of the third dimension would have no concept of the connection I had with Theresa. No one needed to know anyway and anyone interested could read my book. This connection was ours alone - a fifth-dimension connection materializing in the third. We were each other's from a distant time long ago.

We are all souls having an experience living in a physical body, living in the density consciousness of the third dimension where man's lunacy and negativity bombard us daily. I began to realize it was a difficult place to reside in once awakened and decided to distance myself from society as much as possible, giving me an edge on life in the fifth dimension and grounding my first three chakras in the third dimension, while letting my fourth, fifth, sixth and seventh soar higher and higher. Seeking mastery of my soul while in human form was my master plan and of course, Theresa would be the final piece of the puzzle, completing my soul in every way. After all we were two halves of the same soul!

As I continued with my house renovations and preparing for its sale, a trip for supplies was needed. It had been five weeks since I delivered my signed copy to Theresa and feeling her energy quite intensely over the past few days, I decided to pay a visit. Knowing not what to expect, I jumped on the cycle and pedaled north. It was a beautiful day as I cycled toward my familiar feeling of home, following my soul and being guided by my heart.

I walked through those sliding doors once again with ease and grace. They reminded me of the lych

137

gate from my dreams, which I now stood behind at the junction, waiting for the light of the candle-lit lantern to appear.

As we settled in and commenced our conversation I felt our emerging energies had changed. Theresa was different, her energy felt different, her smile radiated the warmest light I have ever seen. She was so beautiful in that moment that once again time was non-existent, and I have never felt more alive in my life as I realized she was the one I had been waiting for my entire life. There had been a shift in her consciousness and this explained her intense energy that I had felt a few days before.

The book of course turned out to be the main topic. She had completed half of it and loved it. I was thrilled. After all my love for her is sprinkled on every page, and as we continued the meeting of our eyes expelled the truth of our connection several times, very intensely I might add. Theresa felt our connection in the 3-D physical realm - the mire was losing its grip. This was a milestone and the book was having an impact on her awakening. Hats off to my team and the universe!

Cooking has been something I have done my entire life and a home-cooked meal is what I enjoy every day. It had been a conversation topic between Theresa and myself on several occasions.

I offered to deliver her a home-cooked meal the following week. She looked up at me smiling, her dark brown eyes capturing my attention as she replied, "I'll be here all week."

I had felt a change within myself that day also. My consciousness had shifted once again. Our conversation and interaction with each other had changed. Our spiritual connection had evolved and was grounding itself on the physical plane, but there was still the karmic partner.

At this point in my journey I was learning to live in the present one moment at a time, leaving the past in the forgotten passages of time. I was freeing myself of the 3-D constructs that society has programmed to be true and letting my soul soar.

The puzzle had begun to paint a portrait portraying my journey. I had been led by the intuition of my heart straight to Theresa. At that moment I had made the conscious decision to continue my high wire walk further out on the limb. This decision was renewed once again with a conscious awareness never felt before. The unconditional love that we shared together within the fifth dimension was starting to find its way into the third and intense as it was, I was learning to live with it. Propelling and fuelling my own self-love, raising my vibration and centering it within my soul, I could feel an alignment taking place and something profound had taken place since my last visit. I seemed to have stepped up to the plate, hit a home run, and ended up back where I had started but with new insights and knowledge.

My house renovations were progressing, and I had prepared Theresa's care package, which I had promised to deliver within the week. So, what better day to deliver than a Monday - the fourteenth of September 2020? The day was overcast and grey, cool and crisp. I boarded and launched the cycle and headed north. I arrived at my destination excited with anticipation of the expected smile, only to be enlightened with news of her absence. A new work schedule had given her the day off. Now previous instantaneous absences of hers were triggers for me and would send me spiraling back down into the quagmire of density within the third dimension, but I was not triggered on this particular day. Intuition informed me that I had mastered another step in my ascension. Leaving the package with a co-worker, I purchased my renovation supplies and cycled south.

September 15/20 - the following morning. While I slept, a familiar voice was heard within my subconscious. My name, Randy, was heard followed by a deep sigh. This was the third time that Theresa had spoken to me within my dream state while sleeping, speaking to me from the fifth dimension. This had happened on two previous occasions, once again confirming our spiritual connection.

The two crystals that Plasoveus had given me unlocked the lych gate and I now stood at the junction of two paths. At the threshold of the bridge I waited for the light of the lantern to appear.

Theresa still had the karmic partner, I had one of the seven deadly sins to eradicate, and our egos, along with the quagmire of 3–D density consciousness were what we faced each day. Wondering what the future would bring, I held my ground, walking further out on the limb.

TWO

FOLLOW – UP

September 19/20. Five twenty-two a.m. Guided information was received for this chapter as thought processes bombarded my mind, giving me insights to share. Old or new, documented or not - it did not matter. All I knew was that it did pertain to my journey and was relevant information for those awakened souls who have commenced the journey home.

People and friends appear and disappear throughout one's life in incarnation after incarnation for all kinds of reasons. It could be to help in some way or even to teach each other a lesson or two. For all facets of life there will always be help in one form or another. Being guided every step of the way, and being aware of the help along the way, is progress toward the soul's mastery while in the third dimension.

The twin flame experience is a very intense spiritual evolution that takes the couple through the mirroring effect of each other. It sheds light on their individual shadows and triggers them to recognize and visit the darkest depths of their souls. Distancing themselves from one another, they search for self-love while they heal past trauma from previous incarnations. Living through intense emotional swings and isolation from society while routinely continuing with their lives, conscious awareness and complete trust in the universe are needed to manifest the union of the couple. This is no easy feat. The twin flame journey is all about mastering the density consciousness of the 3–D physical realm that we all call home, but which is all an illusion.

Living within the illusion through incarnation after incarnation is a hard road for any soul. Learning and advancing our souls in each incarnation until the day arrives and the awakening process begins. We must all remember that we have chosen to experience life in human form and never in earth's history have so many begun to awaken. The evolution of man continues with a shift in human consciousness never seen before that will change humanity forever!

The spiritual evolution of man will test his spirituality and the awakened soul will not be alone. Shaken and wavering, the awakened will travel their individual paths out of the density consciousness of the third dimension into the fifth. Now that the fourth has collapsed, they will live in the fifth while grounded in the third within human form. There they will wait for evolution to take them even further, individually controlling their consciousness and traveling to any dimension at will.

The front-runners of the new earth have now ascended to the fifth dimension, trailblazing a new path and helping the newly awakened. Human evolution is now underway and light workers all around the world are doing their part to help with the ascension of humankind, transmitting information via the World Wide Web.

The web has become the central source of information distribution for the world. There is little control over what is transmitted and all is open to interpretation and clarification. That being said, follow the intuition of your heart and only absorb what resonates with you. Your soul will know the truth. Listen to it! There are many gifted light workers transmitting information through the web but there are also darker forces trying to influence the information. So once again, be aware and diligent, listen to your guidance and follow it with an open heart.

Within the density consciousness of the third dimension, the ego is in the driver's seat controlling man's consciousness, and making him believe that he is always right. This creates a world full of deception and lies until the soul is awakened and the ego takes the back seat as man awakens, one soul at a time, and egos begin to be controlled. Society as we know it will begin to change, not overnight of course, but unhurriedly subtle changes will have the unawakened questioning with disbelief.

Self-love is the number one fundamental requirement for the spiritually awakened and should be practiced each day. Self-love is the first step to compassion and must live within each soul in order to love unconditionally. This is not an easy task for any awakened soul.

Repeated incarnations again and again advancing our souls is a rigorous undertaking to say the least. Experiencing the density consciousness of the 3-D physical realm hinders the soul from flying. With the ego at the helm, they are the schoolyard of hard knocks and Ascension Training 101 in incarnation after incarnation. We collect karma as we continue to evolve and hide it deep within until the soul is awakened and the ascension process begins. Then it is transmuted back into the universe, purging the soul of past traumas and childhood wounds.

The density consciousness of the third dimension in which we live is ego based and fuelled by lower vibrational emotions. The soul must learn to discern between the higher and lower vibrations. Learning to recognize the difference, it can then transmute the lower vibrations back into the universe. In so doing, this is the first step toward controlling one's ego. Always being consciously aware of thoughts passing through one's mind and observing them and what serves no purpose, one can simply let them disappear. Neither judging nor reacting to them, just simply letting them fade away. Being able to control one's ego is mastery of the soul while in human form and hindering its control will let the soul evolve even further. As the evolution of the soul continues, the ego will be completely eradicated and newly incarnated souls will be ego-less.

The illusion of the world begins to become second nature to the awakened as they begin to deprogram from the 3-D constructs of our society. This enables them to detect the lunacy of man and never to be judgmental of others, for those who sleep will also awaken.

Twin souls originate from the splitting of one soul into two, both of which carry the same soul signature and a shared heart space. They live many incarnations within the third dimension, advancing and evolving with every incarnation completed. They search for one another subconsciously until the soul signature of their beloved is found. Their soul signatures merge together, reuniting them once again. Never again can they be separated once the merge is complete. Their journeys begin as twin flames, living in the physical third dimension. Aware of their connection in the fifth dimension, they both heal and prepare for their manifested union in the third dimension where they will be the front runners of the new world, introducing unconditional love to the world through their example, freeing society of its 3-D constructs and introducing a new sacred sexual template for the world to follow.

As man continues to evolve, the awakening process will continue. Some will embrace the process and evolve further, acknowledging their newfound awareness and consciousness, while others will choose to remain in the density consciousness of the third dimension where the judgment of others and lower energies run rampant. Controlled by their egos, they will continue to cause conflict until the incarnation cycle awakens all those living in the third dimension. This will allow society to embrace and practice unconditional love, propelling earth's society into the new millennium, banishing all lower vibrations and frequencies, deleting the ego from the human experience and rewriting 3-D constructs of society. Allowing man's deprogramming to commence will push the envelope of evolution one step beyond the programmed society of the past where everyone was programmed to be like everyone else and follow the same generic guidelines laid out before them, for generation after generation. Never realizing the illusion in which they lived, they focused on materialism and greed!

At the time that I write this book, man's monetary system is alive and well and it will continue to cause chaos within today's society. Its cornerstone of greed will soon diminish as the awakened souls of the world replace the sleepwalkers one by one and through the ascension process usher in a monetary-free society.

I would like to reiterate once again at this time - because this is important to remember - our souls have all chosen to incarnate into human form and live in a world of density consciousness. Learning and advancing their souls in each and every incarnation, returning again and again until they are awakened and the ascension progress begins. This will be the hardest part of man's evolutionary advancement so far.

Merging dimensional energies from all dimensions are causing the awakened soul to absorb more light and a DNA upgrade has commenced. Advancing to twelve-strand DNA is the next evolutionary phase of humanity. For the awakened this will cause ascension symptoms of all varieties ranging from headaches that will be non-localized and cause pressure in one or both ears, sudden movements of energy that physically jolt the body, one's vision my become non-stable and shifting - one day fine, and blurred the next. There may be pressure in the ears along with hearing high-pitched tones, and sensitivity to smell, taste and sound will heightened. Interruptions to sleep patterns will occur in different forms. The guidance received is to just allow your energy to flow - there will be a general sense of free-flowing energy - just let it happen.

Pressure within the chest and heartburn will indicate the galactic heart opening up, embracing an overwhelming love for humanity. Bumping into and dropping things will occur unintentionally and there will be feelings of moving fast and accomplishing more in a shorter period of time. Losing track of time may occur while taking a walk in nature or even multitasking around the house. Anywhere at any time, a lack of attention and focus for any length of time may arise and be noticed with a thought. A need to de-clutter will appear out of the norm along with a new color you are attracted to. Relationship and/or career priorities may change. Public environments may cause discomfort together with revisiting old habits and patterns that were long ago left by the wayside. A change in diet and experimenting with fasting can also occur.

The spiritual awakening process is something that no one has ever experienced before and it will lead the participant to question his or her sanity more than once. Brief suicidal thoughts may arise but are generally disregarded and rejected by the soul.

Recounting the rumor of Vincent Van Gogh - did he commit suicide? This thought has crept quietly through the back door of many awakened twin flames, confirming that they are indeed sane and the twin flame phenomenon is divinely real and insanity is nowhere to be found!

Searching for answers and clarification will set one's mind at ease and erase the thought of insanity, giving your soul some breathing room and a direction of home straight ahead, viewed from the crow's nest of course.

For the awakened twin flame, the spiritual evolution of the awakening process will plunge the participant into times of utter loneliness and isolation. Loneliness is a feature of density consciousness and the awakened will soon realize that he/she is not alone. The spiritual beings are with us twenty-four seven, guiding and protecting us, as is the twin we are never separated from. So, as we expand and shift in consciousness, loneliness will disappear from the timeline that you inhabit. Isolation is a little different to navigate in the third dimension since we are all social animals. The initial isolation from society is usually caused by the loss of friends and family who cannot relate to your awakening insights and spirituality. Finding like-minded people will take the edge off the isolation. We must all remember to pass no judgment on those who sleep for they will awaken in their own time.

As I sat down to write this follow up to the information mentioned in book one, I stayed present within the moment. The moment within the moment, and evaluated where my journey has taken me, where my life has led me and where will my story lead?

The Rolling Stones "WAITING ON A FRIEND" crept into my heart space on two different occasions but not in an icy way. Sending it out to Theresa, I wait at the junction of two paths where we once departed in opposite directions.

THREE

THE – FENCE

The wind howled and its strength removed the stubborn leaves that had remained from the summer of 2020. The colors of yellows, browns and reds littered below where they once hung from the branches of sixty-year-old elm trees. The rumble of the pan was vacant from my ears and the crispness of the air ushered in the month of the dead. Bringing with it a strange occurrence that guided me further toward the candle-lit village of home.

Malachite is a gemstone associated with the heart chakra and spirituality. Opening the heart to love aids in the soul's transformation. While helping to identify what is blocking one's spiritual growth, it is tied to the subconscious and may influence the dreams we have, breaking unwanted ties and old patterns. It is a very versatile stone.

I have a collection of crystals and stones that I use in my daily meditations. One day preparing for a meditation I discovered that my Malachite stone had cracked in half. Now this did seem a little strange but I never gave it a second thought until I was guided to give half to Theresa, and then it made perfect sense.

My house renovations were in full swing and I was busy preparing for the sale of my home. I was multi-tasking projects throughout the house - upgrading this and that, adding a new hot water tank etc. It was a big undertaking but I accepted it while envisioning my new home in Trail. After all, my move was being guided and my spiritual team had my back 24/7. Needing some supplies to further my renovations would be an excellent excuse for a visit, but one was not needed anyway! So, watching the weather I scheduled a warm day - as warm as possible in October anyway.

The weather looked favorable for Tuesday October 6/20, according to the weather network anyway. I would play it by ear and see what transpired. As my eyes began to sense the sunlight of a new day, my restless sleep was forgotten and my day commenced with a grin from ear to ear. Within that instant of a moment my familiar sense of home engulfed my presence, directing me north once again.

I started my day with a glass of water and some vitamins and continued with my newfound fasting routine, which had developed into a way of life. My body had adjusted to eating only once a day. Red meats and chicken had been deleted from my diet and I had eased myself into a plant-based diet and twenty hours between meals was an everyday occurrence. I felt better than I had in years. More energy and stamina came along as a result. My sleep patterns changed and I was able to rest more comfortably. With the free weight program that I had been familiar with for years, my body led the charge giving me assurance to continue. For a lot of the spiritually awakened, diet changes are not uncommon and can be referred to as a sign of awakening.

IF THE WHOLE WORLD ADOPTS VEGETARIANISM IT CAN CHANGE THE DESTINY OF HUMANKIND. ALBERT EINSTEIN

The sun had hit its plateau and the warmest part of the day had begun. Dressing warmly, just as my mother had taught me, I cycled north toward home, Theresa's presence guiding me with every circle the pedals completed. The October sun smiled down as I rode closer to my destination and anticipation grew with tremendous anxiety, followed by complete peacefulness as I walked through those sliding doors once again.

There she was with those captivating deep brown eyes that just pulled me in and confirmed yet again the connection of our past, present and future, all rolled up into the now. Being an empath gives me the ability to feel and sense people's emotions and energies and I knew she was not feeling well. She explained that she'd had a headache most of the day. I thought to myself - Ah! An ascension symptom.

As our conversation continued, I elaborated on the breaking of my Malachite stone. Holding out my hand with the two halves in my palm, she graciously took half. Peering back at me from those beautiful deep brown eyes, like she had so many times before, she smiled with acceptance. For the moment within that moment we both had two feet in the fifth dimension.

I was never so close to home before. The remembrance of a time of separation had crept through a slight opening in time and there I was observing Theresa sitting on a fence - a fence that separated the third and fifth dimensions. Not knowing where to jump, she was torn between the density consciousness of the third dimension and the expanding consciousness of the fifth. I understood her dilemma, knowing that she had come to a pivotal point in her journey; it was two feet in the third or two in the fifth!

I had been faced with this very same dilemma and understood from the experience of my own journey.

Once awakened and the spiritual path is walked upon, no one looks back for long. Like Sodom & Gomorrah, the density consciousness of the third is overwhelming to the awakened!

Sitting on the fence is a giant leap forward in one's ascension progress. After living countless incarnations within the density consciousness of the third dimension which has been the ego's comfort zone, we begin to analyze and question the illusion in which we live. Having spent incarnation after incarnation learning and advancing our souls, the awakened now evolves further and enters another stage of humanity's evolution. Leaving the comfort zone of density consciousness to explore the awareness of their consciousness, controlling their egos while embracing their newfound love for humanity.

The pivotal moment within the timeline Theresa and I travelled together was upon her. All my knowing and intuition told me from our shared heart space that she was ready to explore the fifth with me. Willing to spend more time there and release the density consciousness of the third behind, not looking back any longer but climbing the mainmast towards the crow's nest, her soul was about to fly!

As the evolution of our souls continues to expand and the awareness of consciousness takes flight, our souls yearn for more. The practice of non-judgment of society will propel our souls into the seventh dimension, taking flight to where they have never been before and leading humanity into the golden age of heaven on earth.

For the awakened, time will begin to be more fluid than linear and timeline shifts along with shifts in consciousness happen within the now. The subtleties of these shifts may not be noticed but will surface as one's consciousness expands further.

WISDOM & CLARITY ARE FOUND WITHIN

THE SILENCE OF ONE'S EGO

-RBK

FOUR

PUZZLE PIECES & SHIFTS

My puzzle was progressing slowly with every bit of information that came my way. My spiritual team was busy keeping my questions answered through a variety of information transmissions that at this time in my journey I was quite adept at. Other sources included direct information channeled from Archangels through psychics, via the gift of automatic writing and through directly conversing with them.

Information recently acquired interlocked another piece, giving me one of those a-ha! moments. It explained the origins of twin flames and also some information acquired in my first channeled reading.

There are four soul groups that are reuniting once again after years of incarnations. Reunification is their main objective, and finding the wholeness of their group's own soul energy: Union souls – Multi-expressional – Dual souls and Omni souls. As I continue I will explain the union soul.

The Union soul is one expression. A soul that came out of the Tu'Layan time into the time of the first Atlantis. At the end of the first Atlantis the union soul was literally spilt in half. Producing two halves of the same soul, sharing the same heart space, soul energy and soul signature along with the same chakra system. Each of them set forth on separate journeys, searching for one another for incarnation after incarnation. Eventually finding each other with divine guidance at the helm, their energies merge and the twin flame phenomenon is initiated.

As I navigate this new information and place the puzzle piece into place, the awareness of this information connects the dots to form a question I have asked myself recently: Who is Theresa to me and who am I to her? A question answered and reiterated within my first channeled reading nearly a year ago.

As the reading commenced, Theresa's higher self-relayed a message from the fifth dimension - that she and I had not seen one another for an exceptionally long time and that a reunion was to take place. Yet again, reiterating our connection that dated back to the fall of Atlantis.

This story is not mine alone! This is our story and it could not have been written without her! As a stream of tears begins to fall, I realize I am never alone! And insane I am not! After all we are two halves of the same soul!

The intuition of my heart awoke my soul on the morning of November 2nd/20. The sun was high with a temperature of fifty degrees above zero thanks to global warming – something that many refer to as a cycle. Theresa's energy was like a monkey on my back, enticing me home for a visit and I could never say no to her. I wiped the sleep from my eyes, shaved, dressed and prepared. The feeling of home was calling once again, so I cycled north yet again.

The cool air was brisk as a slight breeze flowed across my freshly shaven face. Dressed warmly I pedaled vigorously until I was warm and all of a sudden home was in view. Locking up the cycle, I approached the familiar sliding doors that opened for me as though I was expected. Crossing the threshold, I could feel the intense negative energies within the building. Taken back for a bit I adjusted to the surroundings and searched for Theresa.

Being informed that she was having lunch, I proceeded to the lunchroom. As I entered, the negative energy was abundant but in amongst all that negative was positive and there she sat. Smiling back at me as our eyes met and engaging in conversation, we were both at home.

As I spend more and more time in the fifth dimension, my awareness of all the egos running rampant in the world, accompanied by attitudes does not surprise me anymore. Being asked to leave triggered me and left me in a state of confusion for a moment, but learning to evaluate situations and pass no judgment keeps one's consciousness and awareness in the fifth dimension.

Theresa and I resumed our conversation at her workstation. It was slow and we both entered our own space. Discussing the book, I pushed her a bit and asked some questions that related to the spirituality of the book. Having not shied away from the questions, Theresa answered insightfully and fired back with some questions herself.

As we spent each moment within the moment together conversing, time was fluid and we each complemented home completely with ease and grace. We peered into each other's eyes, acknowledging the same soul we had shared since the fall of Atlantis.

I knew Theresa was on the spiritual fence and felt her reluctance to place both feet in the fifth dimension, where I waited at the junction holding the candle-lit lantern for her to use as a beacon, leading her home and back into my arms for all eternity.

Sitting on the fence can be arduous, doubt and fear will manifest into what-ifs. "Should I or should I not" will recycle through one's mind, controlled by the ego of course, pulling the participant back to the comfort zone of density consciousness once again, back to the security of the karmic partner and the illusion of the third dimension. This will continue daily as the soul and the ego battle it out on the battlefield within the illusion of density.

Theresa's battle had taken her there and her soul was resting in the crow's nest. Her soul was about to fly! With the battle not over, waiting to shift or be shifted, I replaced a candle in the lantern. For the tears of joy I shed had extinguished the light and for an instant within the moment, she was lost and all of a sudden, a glint of light flashed from her eyes as she removed the malachite stone that I had given her days earlier.

Karmic partner relationships are placed into our charts as catalysts to lessons - to learn from and help advance our souls. We all add them to our incarnation charts before we incarnate and can take some time to accomplish the lessons. Moving on from the karmic and initiating one's soul contract is a giant step forward in the soul's evolution.

At this point in my journey I had become a night owl with absolutely no schedule whatsoever. I was only concerned with the evolution of my soul and manifesting union with Theresa. I had a focused awareness, unwavering commitment and unabridged trust. All was in divine order and timing would be crucial.

Feeling a shift within once again, periods of peacefulness were lengthening. The presence of Theresa had become more stable within the daylight but as daylight faded and darkness fell upon Mother Earth, periods of her intense presence would overwhelm me, making me feel more alive than I have ever felt in my entire life. Welcoming the shift brought new insights along with installed puzzle pieces that led me to understand the four knowns. While lengthening my time spent in the fifth dimension.

ONE – I AM NOT MY BODY

TWO – MY MIND IS MY SERVANT

THREE – I KEEP MY EYES ON THE DIVINE ALL THE TIME

FOUR – ALL IS IN DIVINE ORDER

I soon understood that practicing the knowns helped me to shift once again, pushing the evolution of my soul even further. With more clarity than ever before I began to remember who I really was! Speaking my truth and following my soul, guided by the intuition of my ascended heart, I was in flow with the universe. Holding my hand out and waiting for Theresa to accept my invitation, I had become immersed in my own oneness, watching myself move forward through this incarnation through the lens of an eight-millimeter movie projector. Manifesting the future every step of the way.

My thirst for spiritual knowledge was increasing. Now on a conscious level, my awareness was leading my conscious mind to follow. Both in sync with each other, my soul began to soar to higher heights enabling me to view my thoughts more easily than before - only using what serves my purpose.

It had been twenty-one months since I had been catapulted into the eye of the tempest, and Theresa being the catalyst within the center, sent me efferently searching the new realm I had been launched into.

Living in the fifth dimension where time is fluid instead of linear changed all perspective of time that I was used to in the third, and twenty-one months seemed like yesterday to me. Flipping the calendar, the big block letters spelled out November, and made me quiver at the thought of winter. Knowing that a long separation from home was inevitable any day, I set forth more healing toward the fated polarity shift in our soul signature energy that would bring us closer to union.

The seventh was the dreaded day that dawned my quivering into reality with an accumulation of wet snow. Too heavy to shovel and leaving a thin layer of ice underneath, I glanced through my back-door window. Flakes as big as thumb nails floated to the ground, piling one upon another. I brewed a cup of red tea, sat in front of the keyboard and continued to document my story - authentic, raw and real - straight from my heart, I continued. The pan head was silent. Once again, an echo of a tear was heard as it hit the floor.

I bathed in the peacefulness that seemed to have entered my own little world, engulfing my aura, and gave thanks to all in the realm that sent it in my direction, enabling the navigation of my days and nights more easily than before. Keeping the broken malachite stone close, I continued to write.

165

Strengthening my newfound peacefulness, it was a keep-sake that seldom left my side, reminding me once again of the spiritual connection Theresa and I shared. I envisioned the spring of 2021, the warming sun melting the snow, the fresh smell of spring as the snow turned to liquid, knowing that the season change would lead me back home once again, a short cycle ride north.

Shaken from my vision of spring, mid-November was easing in the entrance of winter with short bursts of snowfall and increments of temperature drop. Demanding that we all beware of what was upon us, and from my memory, so clear just like yesterday and all the previous years, I was so aware! I battened down all that needed to be, turned up the furnace and continued with book number three.

FIVE

NOVEMBER-DECEMBER 2020

SUMMATION

The fluidity of time had caught me unaware. I was too busy to grow old and living in the fifth dimension initiated reverse ageing to all those awakening souls who were keeping their eyes on the divine at all times! This indeed did catch my awareness.

November was ending and December would undoubtedly bring with it some melancholy. The reason would be obvious of course, but with my newfound peacefulness, the charted waters ahead would be smooth for the most part. With my house renovation nearly complete I would start to concentrate on more de-cluttering and packing, which would keep me focused on the move to Trail.

The puzzle at this point was putting itself together and I felt comfortable with my journey. Knowing that all was in divine order I continued to follow my heart, led by my intuition. Never second-guessing any discussion whatsoever, my life change was supported by the universe. Complete trust being the foundation of all forward movement, my path was visible and clear. I was learning to navigate the fifth dimension more and more each day and had my sights on the seventh.

In a sense my world was like a cloud. Viewing the world in which I lived from a distance, the fifth dimension of course, focusing on what served my purpose and letting go of what did not, I began to wonder whether any of my neighbors had awakened.

I began to draw inwards, embracing my newfound self. I discovered a whole new world that was always there, a world where I could master the density of the third dimension while placing both feet in the fifth. This became more and more familiar to me as each day passed.

The fluidity of time in which I now lived and understood, enabled me to shed my previous characters of KR and Tall, which made space for my new authentic self to take up residence, who had always been there but had been shadowed by ego - hidden away and trapped until my awakening on that fated day when Theresa entered my life.

As I write these words and the ink swells the page, I embrace her energy yet again. Recollecting the year 1978, I really love you - an Ian Thomas song flashes through the portal of my mind, bringing with it that intense love that originates in the fifth dimension. One that our higher selves have shared since Atlantis.

As I continued to document my journey, the calendar will be flipped yet again and December twenty 20 will be ushered in. Twenty-one months had seemingly passed me by. With another Christmas around the corner I called upon my spiritual team. Sending forth a cry from my heart, I asked for one Christmas gift that would ease the melancholy that was rippling the waters, one that I had chartered until the end of the year. Speaking straight from my heart with sincerity I humbly asked for some time alone with Theresa.

As I stirred within my dream state on the morning of December first, I was once again at home in the fifth dimension where my consciousness was 24 / 7. While my etheric body grounded itself on the earth plane, Theresa's arms wrapped around my upper body as we lay together and our higher selves merged, visiting each other in the dream state of the fifth dimension. This was not unusual or unexpected and was beginning to become a regular occurrence. The cry from my heart had been answered.

With the sunrise each day, my focal point of the day would be focused on my spiritual journey and on Theresa of course. Blending day and night together as the numbers grew larger on the December page of the calendar, twenty 21 would be a year of mastery choice.

I was the spiritual twin, while Theresa the matrix twin took refuge while drawing a line in the sand. She observed both sides, the 3–D side in which the security of density consciousness and the karmic partner were familiar and comfortable, and glanced from time to time toward the 5–D side to the unfamiliarity of awareness but the knowing of home where I now resided full time. Conscious and navigating both dimensions I was beginning to soar. Knowing that the choice before her would eventually lead to our union, reminded me of Liz's reading and I smiled, knowing all was in Divine order.

As my years accumulate and the larger digits represent a number that the young refer to as old, I smile, grin and smirk, for the most important part of my life lies ahead of me. Being in complete control, with my eyes on the divine at all times, the awareness of my consciousness is honed and my intuition is as sharp as a tack. Once again, the words resurface - all is in divine order!

December first / 20. My fluttering eyes focused in on the dimness of my basement where I prefer to rest my soul when the sun hides its light from the earth. Rested and ready to start my day, I hit start on the computer, logged in, and checked my mail. My astonished eyes, still adjusting to the brightness of the morning sun, caught a glimpse of the word congratulations.

Literary Titan, a review and promotional company that I had been using to promote my book had also reviewed my book and it was therefore entered into that year's book awards. What a wonderful surprise - my book, or should I say our book, had received Literary Titan's silver book award along with five-star reviews. I was over the moon and the next couple of days were filled with immense gratitude, sent forth to Theresa and every being in the realm. This event did clarify that our spiritual connection was manifesting some special events and drew me closer to her more than ever, confirming once again that all was in divine order.

I wanted to inform Theresa of the win but intuition enlightened me to hold off for the moment and within the next moment all was clear. I would deliver the news with the manuscript of the second book that was nearing completion. Being informed that she was

171

interested in reading the second installment, I would proceed with plan A. December had ushered in another shift of my consciousness that was not subtle in anyway. No! More like the roar of a lion.

Living outside the box and being an introverted rebel, navigating a world in which many a set of eyes had been rolled in my direction was all in preparation for my awakening, and then the time was manifested as I surfed a new timeline. There she was, a strand of hair hung over her face to one side, and at that moment I was reminded of the past. Together thrust into the eye of a hurricane where time did not exist, and in that moment within the moment we were propelled into a search for answers leading to self.

Theresa, still on the fence, was aware that the choice she would inevitably have to make would undoubtedly change her life. It was a road into the future that only her soul would know. Would she follow or remain on the fence? Would she listen to her soul and follow her heart? Straddling the world of density consciousness and a new beginning, she see-sawed. I held my hand out in invitation, the malachite stone within its palm, waiting at the junction for my beloved.

It was December 19/20 and another piece of the puzzle had been placed. Plasoveus was also guiding Theresa on her journey.

The twelve days of Christmas for me were intense and emotional. My second book was nearing completion and 20/20 was nearing its close. My flip phone had been silent and the quiet of the holiday had ushered in a thought. The quietness of one's mind is hard to find and harder yet, someone to quiet it.

Patience is key to anyone travelling the twin flame path but patience is fleeting and soon evolves into unwavering trust. Knowing that all is in divine order, realizing that moving forward is the only option, I had come to this point in my journey and understood that Theresa would awaken when she was ready.

The teeter-totter on which she rode was still touching down on both sides of the fence and she knew not where to place her feet. Briefly spending time on both sides, her preference was still the security of the karmic partner within the density of mass consciousness that I refused to frequent.

Time as we know it does not exist in the realms and my consciousness had adapted to circular time where I could see only moment to moment. Glimpses of the future would invade my dreams while my visions became more intense and personal. In sighting information about a life to unfold with Theresa, guided and controlled by the realms, sending me all that I needed to know, I continued forward.

December 28/20. Christmas had run its course and my yearly calendar would need to be changed. Sun and cloud joined me as I hiked to my destination. Theresa entertained my consciousness throughout my lengthy hike. While returning home with calendar in hand, I recalled the previous year. Van Gogh's painting A Starry Night, flashed through my mind, followed by the welcoming smile of my friend.

Twenty 20 had abruptly transported me to the thirtieth of December and there I was. It had seemed as though I had travelled through time. The passing year was a blur, disappearing and taking with it my old template, my old self. Leaving my authentic new self to forge ahead and never look back. Time was spiraling now and the vortex was pulling me straight through the center, like an arrow released from a long bow, spinning straight through the center. The past was irrelevant and the present was lived in the moment. The future was predestined and fate held my hand. As I placed each foot ahead of the other I would manifest all my desires and dreams in twenty 21. Theresa would of course be at the forefront of the future.

My spiritual pilgrimage had been arduous to say the least but intense and glorious as well. I was well aware that Theresa would be the final piece of the puzzle. We were both woven into the tapestry of time where the twin flame phenomenon is absolutely real!

I had made no plans for New Year's Eve. I was beside myself - twenty 21 would be the year of the phoenix. From out of the ashes, I would soar to new heights. I had been buried too long. Major life changes had been set in motion within the past year. I would embrace them all and follow through. My transformation was coming around full circle. My authentic-self had emerged, acknowledging that I was a light being having an experience in human form and had evolved.

My heart undeniably knows that Theresa will write the epilogue to our story. She was, has been, is, and will continue to be, the driving force behind my soul's evolution and without her there would be no story. Once again, I have written these words for HER!

As the last hour closes in and 20 twenty-one approaches, the keystrokes begin to fade. With an appropriate song from Linda Ronstadt "Lose Again", the keystrokes are silent. Happy New Year Theresa.

-BEGOTTEN TIME-

EACH MOMENT – EVERY SECOND

EACH MINUTE – EVERY HOUR

OF EVERY DAY

WAS FOR HER.

SINCE THE LAST SUN SET ON ATLANTIS

SHE HAS BEEN MINE

AND I HER'S

TWO HALVES OF THE SAME SOUL.

SEPARATED

UNTIL NOW.

TIME WAS

BEGOTTEN FOR HER AND I.

UNTIL NOW.

-R.B.K.

EPILOGUE

As I stepped forth into 2021, Twenty-20 left me more aware. My consciousness had shifted, peacefulness had become a close friend and I had surrendered to the divine. Knowing that all was in divine order, I kept my eyes on the divine at all times. With unwavering trust, never gazing at the past, travelling toward my destination: The arms of my beloved Theresa.

Dr. Wayne Dyer left some very inspirational words for humanity before he travelled on: SHIFT OR BE SHIFTED! And I would rather shift than be shifted!

Reviews of this read can be directed to Amazon or Goodreads.

THANK YOU FOR READING

GLOSSARY

ARMAGNAC - BRANDY

BLOCK HEAD - MOTOR

BUILD – A BIKE PROJECT

CABBAGE - MONEY

CHOPPER - CUSTOM MOTORCYCLE

CHOP - MOTORCYCLE

CONE KNUCKLE - CUSTOM ENGINE

CROW'S NEST – LOOKOUT POINT ON A SHIP

CUT - VEST

FXR - HARLEY MODEL

HARDTAIL - MOTORCYCLE FRAME WITHOUT A REAR SUSPENSION

INNIS - BEER

MILL – REFERRING TO A MOTOR

MORPHEUS – GOD OF DREAMS

OIL JOINT – MARIJUANA OIL MIXED WITH MARIJUANA OR

TOBACCO

PAN HEAD - DISCONTINUED ENGINE

RIP - OUT FOR A RIDE

RUB – RICH URBAN BIKER

SHARP FINGER – KNIFE

SHINE – ALCHOL ILLEGALLY DISTILLED

SHVL – DISCONTINUED ENGINE

SPLIFF – MARIJUANA CIGARETTE

SUPER G – CARBURATOR

WICK – HAND THROTTLE

AN

R

B

K

READ

Lightning Source UK Ltd.
Milton Keynes UK
UKHW021919150621
385583UK00002B/304